SEW & SERGE
TERRIFIC TEXTURES

OTHER BOOKS
AVAILABLE FROM CHILTON
Robbie Fanning, Series Editor

Contemporary Quilting

Appliqué the Ann Boyce Way
Barbara Johannah's Crystal Piecing
The Complete Book of Machine Quilting, second edition,
    by Robbie and Tony Fanning
Contemporary Quilting Techniques, by Pat Cairns
Fast Patch, by Anita Hallock
Fourteen Easy Baby Quilts, by Margaret Dittman
Machine-Quilted Jackets, Vests, and Coats, by Nancy Moore
Pictorial Quilts, by Carolyn Vosburg Hall
Precision Pieced Quilts Using the Foundation Method,
    by Jane Hall and Dixie Haywood
Quick-Quilted Home Decor with Your Bernina, by Jackie Dodson
Quick-Quilted Home Decor with Your Sewing Machine,
    by Jackie Dodson
The Quilter's Guide to Rotary Cutting, by Donna Poster
Quilts by the Slice, by Beckie Olson
Scrap Quilts Using Fast Patch, by Anita Hallock
Speed-Cut Quilts, by Donna Poster
Stitch 'n' Quilt, by Kathleen Eaton
Super Simple Quilts, by Kathleen Eaton
Teach Yourself Machine Piecing and Quilting, by Debra Wagner
Three-Dimensional Appliqué, by Jodie Davis
Three-Dimensional Pieced Quilts, by Jodie Davis

Craft Kaleidoscope

Creating and Crafting Dolls, by Eloise Piper and Mary Dilligan
Fabric Painting Made Easy, by Nancy Ward
How to Make Cloth Books for Children, by Anne Pellowski
Jane Asher's Costume Book
Quick and Easy Ways with Ribbon, by Ceci Johnson
Learn Bearmaking, by Judi Maddigan
Shirley Botsford's Daddy's Ties
Soft Toys for Babies, by Judi Maddigan
Stamping Made Easy, by Nancy Ward
Too Hot To Handle? Potholders and How to Make Them,
    by Doris L. Hoover

Creative Machine Arts

ABCs of Serging, by Tammy Young and Lori Bottom
The Button Lover's Book, by Marilyn Green
Claire Shaeffer's Fabric Sewing Guide
The Complete Book of Machine Embroidery,
    by Robbie and Tony Fanning
Creative Nurseries Illustrated, by Debra Terry and Juli Plooster
Distinctive Serger Gifts and Crafts,
    by Naomi Baker and Tammy Young
The Fabric Lover's Scrapbook, by Margaret Dittman
Friendship Quilts by Hand and Machine, by Carolyn Vosburg Hall
Gail Brown's All-New Instant Interiors
Gifts Galore, by Jane Warnick and Jackie Dodson
Hold It! How to Sew Bags, Totes, Duffels, Pouches, and More,
    by Nancy Restuccia

How to Make Soft Jewelry, by Jackie Dodson
Innovative Serging, by Gail Brown and Tammy Young
Innovative Sewing, by Gail Brown and Tammy Young
The New Creative Serging Illustrated,
    by Pati Palmer, Gail Brown, and Sue Green
*Owner's Guide to Sewing Machines, Sergers, and Knitting
Machines*, by Gale Grigg Hazen
Petite Pizzazz, by Barb Griffin
Putting on the Glitz, by Sandra L. Hatch and Ann Boyce
Quick Napkin Creations, by Gail Brown
Second Stitches: Recycle as You Sew, by Susan Parker
Serge a Simple Project, by Tammy Young and Naomi Baker
Sew Any Patch Pocket, by Claire Shaeffer
Sew Any Set-In Pocket, by Claire Shaeffer
Sew Sensational Gifts, by Naomi Baker and Tammy Young
Sew, Serge, Press, by Jan Saunders
Sewing and Collecting Vintage Fashions, by Eileen MacIntosh
Simply Serge Any Fabric, by Naomi Baker and Tammy Young
Singer Instructions for Art Embroidery and Lace Work
Soft Gardens: Make Flowers with Your Sewing Machine,
    by Yvonne Perez-Collins
The Stretch & Sew Guide to Sewing on Knits, by Ann Person
Twenty Easy Machine-Made Rugs, by Jackie Dodson

Know Your Sewing Machine Series,
by Jackie Dodson

Know Your Bernina, second edition
Know Your Brother, with Jane Warnick
Know Your Elna, with Carol Ahles
Know Your New Home, with Judi Cull and Vicki Lyn Hastings
Know Your Pfaff, with Audrey Griese
Know Your Sewing Machine
Know Your Singer
Know Your Viking, with Jan Saunders
Know Your White, with Jan Saunders

Know Your Serger Series,
by Tammy Young and Naomi Baker

Know Your baby lock
Know Your Pfaff Hobbylock
Know Your Serger
Know Your White Superlock

Star Wear

Embellishments, by Linda Fry Kenzle
Make It Your Own, by Lori Bottom and Ronda Chaney
Sweatshirts with Style, by Mary Mulari

Teach Yourself to Sew Better,
by Jan Saunders

A Step-by-Step Guide to Your Bernina
A Step-by-Step Guide to Your New Home Sewing Machine
A Step-by-Step Guide to Your Sewing Machine

SEW & SERGE

TERRIFIC TEXTURES

Jackie Dodson
Jan Saunders

Chilton Book Company
Radnor, Pennsylvania

Published in Radnor, Pennsylvania 19089, by Chilton Book
Company

Designed by Publication Design
Photography by Wyckoff Commercial

Manufactured in the United States of America

ISBN 0-8019-8526-9

A Cataloging-in-Publication record for this book is available from
the Library of Congress.

1 2 3 4 5 6 7 8 9 0   5 4 3 2 1 0 9 8 7 6

Contents

CHAPTER 5
Texturing A to Z
More Than Twenty-Five Techniques to Try

Foreword

This book is about change. Change in the sewing and serging machinery we use, and the way we use it. Change in the way we use and manipulate fabrics, threads, and trims. New feet, new stitches, new fabrics, new machines—all enable us to create increasingly beautiful and complex garments.

Because the sewing and serging possibilities are now so vast, Jackie and Jan have created *Sew & Serge Terrific Textures* to help the modern sew-er use the wonderful new techniques and technologies that have developed in the 1990s. With their book, we may explore new approaches to old designs; use new equipment for old patterns; combine several techniques considered incompatible into one project; or use a ready-made garment as a base for further manipulation and embellishment.

For inspiration, Jackie and Jan invited many designers and artists in the sewing profession to demonstrate their expertise. May their designs, plus those by Jackie and Jan, inspire you to create your own unique garments and projects using your machines to the maximum. May they entice you to experiment with new tools, techniques, and equipment. And may the excitement they create motivate you to continue sewing with a creative approach. Change can be fun!

Linda McGehee

What is the *Sew & Serge* book series?

Terrific Textures is one of the kickoff books in our new *Sew & Serge* series. (*Sew & Serge Pillows! Pillows! Pillows!* is the other.) We hope you'll be inspired by the many ideas and new applications we've discovered during our brainstorming, researching, and writing. You'll also love the exciting, cutting-edge techniques top industry designers contributed to our efforts.

We work with the sewing machine and serger in tandem, because it shortens construction time, makes us more efficient (it's like using the microwave and conventional oven in cooking), and gives us two creative mediums to work in. But we also know that not everyone has a serger, so our instructions are written for both pieces of equipment (similar to recipes and instructions for preparing convenience foods with conventional and microwave ovens).

We use icons to indicate which machine (if any) is needed for the techniques used in each project. This icon 🧵 means the technique requires a serger, this icon 🧵 means a sewing machine will be needed, and this icon (S̶E̶W̶) means neither machine is required. If the technique can be done with either machine, both icons are listed 🧵 or 🧵 . In *Sew & Serge Terrific Textures,* the icons appear in a Texturing Techniques Box at the beginning of each project (see the Introduction for more information).

The *Sew & Serge* books are filled with ideas, inspiration, and easy-to-do projects. In fact, we've organized our easy, easier, and easiest projects so that the easiest one in each chapter comes first. That way, you can sample a technique or concept with a minimum of time and effort. We hope that, regardless of your skill level, you'll enjoy our *Sew & Serge* projects—not only because they fill a need for a gift or will help complete a room, enhance an occasion, or accent an outfit, but also because they're fun. We've tried to respect your budget and busy schedule by offering projects that can be completed in one sitting. We've also been careful to give you the best way to create a project or stitch a technique, rather than including methods just because they're possible. If you like to explore short subjects in greater depth, as we do, give the *Sew & Serge* approach a try.

As we continue our creative adventures, we'd like to hear from you. Do you have an idea for a short-subject sewing or crafting book? Do you have a tip to share? Write to us in care of *Sew & Serge* development: 934 Meadow Crest Road, La Grange Park, IL 60526.

Acknowledgments

Thank you to the people who supplied us with fabulous sewing and serging equipment and for their continued support of our creative endeavors. Without them, this book and the subject of fabric texturing would not exist: Nancy Auch from Tacony Corporation (Baby Lock, Esanté, Éclipse, Simplicity, and Riccar brands); Jane Burbach and Andrea Nynas from Elna, Inc. (Elna, ElnaLock, and Elnita brands); Sue Hausmann and Nancy Jewell from V.W.S., Inc. (Viking, Huskylock, White, and Superlock brands); JoAnn Pugh-Gannon and Gayle Hillert from Bernina of America, Inc. (Bernina and Bernette brands); Sue Thornton from New Home Sewing Machine Company (MyLock and Combi brands); and Linnette Whicker from Pfaff American Sales (Pfaff and Hobbylock brands).

Many thanks to Mary Griffin from Singer Sewing Company for her expert advice on stabilizers; and to April Dunn who represents Signature Thread and Y.L.I.; Joyce Drexler from Sulky of America; Meta Hoge from Coats & Clark; Susan Rock from Madeira; Sharee Dawn Roberts from Web of Thread, whose threads, cords, and fibers made our textures and those contributed by the designers most beautiful. We also want to thank Gutermann, Mettler Metrosene, and Tinsel for their all-purpose sewing, serging, and speciality threads; C.M. Offray for its ribbons; Quality Braid Corp./Sequins International, Inc. for its cross-locked beads; and Wright's Trims for additional trim and textures used in our projects.

Thanks also to Aleene's, Dritz Corporation, Handler Textile Corporation, Kittrich, Palmer/Pletsch, Pellon, Sulky of America, and Therm O Web. Although you can't see their products, their stabilizers, fusible webs, glues, seam sealants, and fabric laminates helped keep our textures smooth and pucker free, and enhanced our raised textures when we needed them to be.

Thank you, Gail Brown, for your idea to have a Designer's Showcase. Just a phone call away, you're always available to listen, advise, help, and be a good friend to both of us. And to the designers who contributed so generously of their time, talent, and materials (and broke speed records making their textures and getting them to us), our thanks to the following: Nancy Bednar, Sandra Benfield, Lynn Browne, Mary Carollo, Deborah Casteel, Diana Cedolia, Amy Doggett, Joyce Drexler, April Dunn, Marilyn Gatz, Gretchen Heinlein-Wilson, Michele Hester, Angie Jachimowski, Grace Johnson, Jill McCloy, Linda McGehee, Cathie Moore, Dori Nanry, Jan Nunn, Joellen Reinhardt, Susan Rock, Patsy Shields, and Linnette Whicker.

Thank you, Robbie Fanning, our editor, for keeping us busy, sane, and for always convincing us we can do anything.

Thank you to our families, who may not have time to read this — they've taken over holidays and other household jobs for us so we can sew, serge, and write.

Introduction

Everybody's doing it. . .fabric texturing that is. From the elegant clothing in designer salons to the comfortable casual wear in the large mass-merchandising discount stores, almost everything is decorated with appliqués, paint, medallions, embroidery, lace, beads, buttons, sequins, and glitz. Often we think we can do it better, make it cheaper, or more creatively. After all, the supplies we need to vent our creative urges are aging, like fine wine, in our own sewing treasure chests. So we were thrilled when the creative juices started flowing for *Terrific Textures*, because it gave us an excuse to experiment with new techniques, with new treatments of old techniques, and with many new products we've wanted to try.

Do you remember opening your first box of crayons? All those colors, so little time. This is the way we feel with our thread and fiber collections as we begin the creative process. We start with color, playing with the possibilities and then choosing a color scheme. Soon our efforts evolve into a combination of textures created by thread, fabric, and cut-out or raised surface design. Making textures is truly creative because you start with a simple base fabric and by cutting it, manipulating it, or adding decoration to it, you create new fabric—terrific textures that never before existed.

When we started, we had hundreds of great ideas. . .in our minds. Then, when we thought of the work involved in creating enough textured yardage to make a garment from scratch, we tended to put the idea on the back burner until we had more time. Then it came to us. . . why don't we leave the tedious garment construction to someone else and save the fun of creating for ourselves? So the texturing projects in *Sew & Serge Terrific Textures* are designed to be made small so you can decorate ready-made clothing—a shirt, jacket, pocket, yoke, cuff, or hem edge—in one sitting.

True to the title of this series, most of the projects in this book incorporate both sewing and serging. In each project there is a **Texturing Techniques Box** that *lists all of the techniques used in the project* and *groups them by machine.* If you need a serger to create a certain effect, you'll see this icon . If you need a sewing machine, you'll see this icon . If either machine can be used, the icons will be shown in combination (or), while this icon (**SEW**) means the project can be done without any machine work (what we call a "no-sew project").

The Texturing Techniques Box also provides *page references for techniques not spelled out within the project*. Directions for many basic techniques are listed alphabetically in Chapter Five: Texturing A to Z. When one of these basic techniques is included in a project, it is listed, along with its page reference, in the Texturing Techniques Box.

For example, in the Slap-Dash and Patch project on page 24, satin stitching is used around the patches. Satin stitching is listed in the Texturing Techniques Box as a technique that can be done with the sewing machine 🧵, and that is explained on page 74. When satin stitching is mentioned in the directions, a quick reference to the Texturing Techniques Box is given so that you can easily find the page in Chapter Five that describes the technique more fully. We hope this will make the instructions less repetitive and a breeze to follow (especially once you've mastered a few of the basic texturing methods).

We hope our ideas act as creative springboards for your texturing projects. Here's a preview. Read them in order or jump around—the easiest techniques are at the beginning of each chapter. Color photographs of the projects (as well as the exciting Designer Showcase) can be found in the color pages of the book.

Chapter One: Easy Openings — Cut-Through, See-Through, and No-Sew Textures gives you four super-easy texturing ideas. Learn:
- how to doodle with and add color to dimensional gel on a project called Zippy Doodles
- the easiest cutwork known to woman (or man) using an exciting new product called Fiber-Etch, which burns away plant fibers, on the When-You-Don't-Like-To-Turn-Corners Cutwork Vest
- a new twist on reverse appliqué we call Petroglyph Pets
- how Can-Can net and colorful buttons create a see-through rainbow in the Peek-A-Button Vest

In Chapter Two we explore sewing and serging Simple Surface Transformations — Textures Applied Flat To The Fabric. Learn:
- how to stitch satin-stitch bars, blobs, and circles, as well as how to couch serger braid, in a piece called Breaking the Boundaries
- how to take the scraps from your sewing room floor, wave-cut them, apply them to a surface, and go Scrap Happy
- how to couch serger braid and other loose fabric, thread, and trim to make the Scrap-Saver's Removable Yoke

- how to weave a variety of cut, sewn, and serged fabric strips, then granite-stitch over the texture to attach it to the project when you make Warp-and-Woof Wear
- how to patch a shirt, whether it has holes in it or not, to make Slap-Dash and Patch
- the easiest, most foolproof way to turn back the edge of a blanket-stitched appliqué in a piece called Curves and Corners

Chapter Three: Transcending the Surface—Textures Raised Above the Fabric will teach you to love raising your textures "above" the fabric. Learn:
- a new angle on Italian cording in The Easy-Angle Italian
- how to let serged squares spill over a denim shirt with Helter Skelter Serged Squares
- how easy it is to do yarn embroidery by making It's-A-Miracle
- a faster and easier way to apply blooms to the surface rather than cutting through the fabric with Flowering Denim

Chapter Four: Tools, Trappings, and Other Tips — A Terrific Textures Tutorial will help you stock your sewing supplies and learn a few tricks that will assist you in your texturing efforts. This chapter also covers how to care for your textured creations.

As mentioned earlier, Chapter Five: Texturing A to Z serves as almost a glossary of many basic texturing techniques. There are more than twenty-five techniques to try, and they are arranged alphabetically, with complete instructions for each technique listed.

For additional inspiration, don't miss the tempting textures in the Designer Showcase, a gallery of five color photos in the middle of the color pages. There you can admire the work of twenty-five talented designers who generously donated their time and efforts to make textures for this book. Learn more about the designers and their work in their own words in the Designer Showcase Key at the back of the book. Their artistry and efforts are certain to inspire your texturing endeavors.

There you have it, an overview of the texturing techniques you'll learn through *Sew & Serge Terrific Textures*. We know you'll enjoy the many tricks, tips, tidbits, and new twists on texturing you'll find on every page.

Happy texturing,
J. D. and J. S.

SEW & SERGE
TERRIFIC TEXTURES

Chapter 1

EASY OPENINGS

Cut-Through, See-Through, and No-Sew Textures

Texturing is not just adding fabric or trim to a base fabric. It's also cutting fabric away — sometimes leaving a see-through hole, sometimes revealing another layer of fabric. This "cutting edge" principle operates in the When-You-Hate-to-Turn-Corners Cutwork Vest and Petroglyph Pets.

We included the Peek-A-Button Vest in this chapter because see-through textures don't always have to be cut out. This one is sewn and filled up. The Zippy Doodles project uses a fun texturing technique that requires neither sewing nor adding fabric.

ZIPPY DOODLES

We added Liquid Beads by Plaid to a ready-made shirt. It's so simple, children and adults alike will have fun with it. Add zip to any plain piece of clothing with your own doodles or use our designs for some creative assistance.

TEXTURING TECHNIQUES

~~SEW~~ **Transferring Designs with Ease** .. p. 77

~~SEW~~ **Foiling**

~~SEW~~ **Sealing**

~~SEW~~ **Using Dimensional Bond**

Fig. 1.1:
Zippy Doodle Shirt.

You'll Need:

Fabric

- Clean and pressed ready-made shirt, jacket, or top (we pre-shrunk our shirt three times, then took it to the laundry to have it washed and pressed again so the surface was smooth and flat)

Kit Materials

- Instruction sheet
- Dimensional bond (gel)
- Liquid Beads Press & Peel Foil Beginner Stud Kit or comparable product
- Silver press-and-peel foil sealer, and applicator (available at your local craft store)

Miscellaneous

- Toothpick
- White disappearing chalk
- Shirt board (available through your local craft store) or plastic-covered cardboard or plastic-coated freezer paper (available at your local food market)

To Texture:

1. Slip the shirt or top over a shirt board to keep the surface flat for drawing and to prevent the dimensional gel from soaking through. If you don't have a shirt board, Nancy Ward, author of *Fabric Painting Made Easy* (Chilton, 1993), recommends using plastic-coated freezer paper. Place the shiny side of the freezer paper on the wrong side of the shirt and iron it on with a dry iron, bonding it to the inside of the garment before you begin decorating it.

2. Trace and transfer the Zippy Doodle designs at the end of this chapter to the shirt using the disappearing chalk or a heat-transfer pen (see Texturing Techniques Box), then go back and add dots and circles in between.

3. Following the manufacturer's instructions, apply dimensional bond (gel) from the bottle, covering the chalk or transfer lines.

Work on one surface of the project at a time. Let the gel dry until it is transparent and sticky.

4. Add the silver foil by placing the foil side of the paper on top of the sticky surface and pressing with your fingers. Pull off the paper. If needed, go back over any spots not covered with foil, using a toothpick to press the paper to the base of the sticky line.
5. Finish your zippy doodles by sealing the foil with the sealer. If you forget this step, the foil will fall off when washed. Let your doodles dry for 72 hours before washing. To care for your project, hand-wash it and lay it flat to dry. *Note:* We used Liquid Beads for the foiling and found the product to work well. However, there are undoubtedly suitable substitutes available through your local craft, fabric, or sewing retailers or mail-order sources.

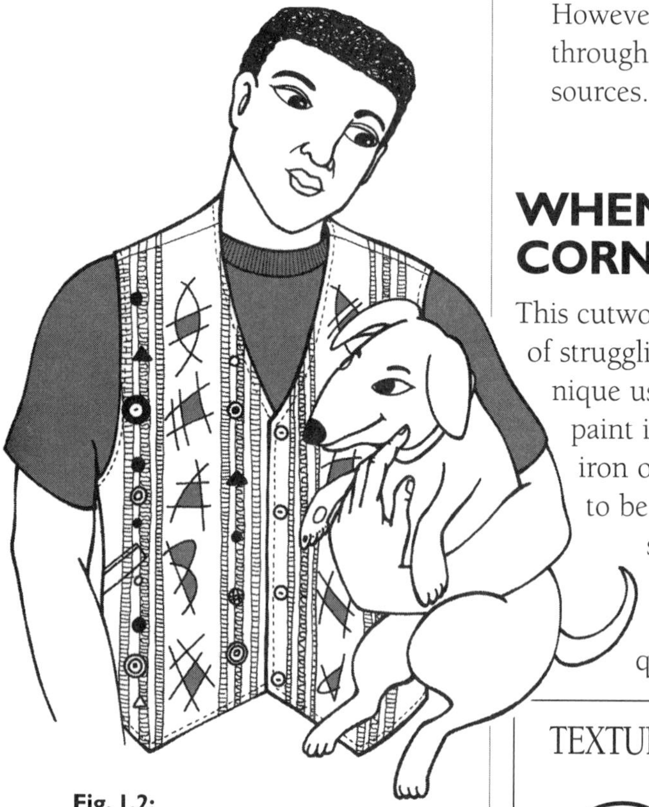

Fig. 1.2:
When-You-Hate-To-Turn-Corners Cutwork Vest.

WHEN-YOU-HATE-TO-TURN-CORNERS CUTWORK VEST

This cutwork project is a variation of the traditional method. Instead of struggling with cutting corners and other tricky points, this technique uses a chemical gel that dissolves plant fibers. You just paint it on the fabric to be removed, allow it to dry, and then iron over it. Use only cotton, linen, or rayon fabric for the area to be removed and synthetic (100% polyester or acrylic) or silk thread for the stitching around the area. Because non-plant fibers aren't harmed by the gel, only the fabric will fall away — with no cutting! What a great look and quick gift ... if you can part with it.

TEXTURING TECHNIQUES

- **The Trace-Over Transfer-Design Method** ..... p. 78
- **Removing Fabric from Inside of Shapes**
- **Fabric-Painting Shapes (optional)**
- **Satin and Decorative Stitch Strategy** .... p. 74
- **Button Sewing—But Not by Hand** .... p. 62
- **Flatlocking Most Fabulous (optional)** .... p. 67

You'll Need:

Fabric
- One starched striped all-cotton vest or starched striped all-cotton fabric to make vest from scratch and vest pattern

Needle
- 90/14 jeans

Thread
- *Top:* black polyester sewing, all-acrylic, or silk embroidery thread
- *Bobbin:* black polyester darning or polyester all-purpose sewing thread

Presser Feet
- Embroidery/appliqué
- Button sewing

Stabilizer
- Water-soluble

Miscellaneous
- Disappearing marker
- Paper towels
- 36 assorted black buttons
- Iron
- Black permanent marker
- Dressmaker's carbon and ballpoint pen
- Bottle of Fiber-Etch Fabric Remover (available through local sewing machine dealers and mail-order sources)

To Texture:

1. Transfer Cutwork designs at the end of this chapter using dressmaker's carbon and empty ballpoint pen (see Texturing Techniques Box). Darken carbon lines with disappearing marker.

2. Back each design with water-soluble stabilizer. Set your sewing machine for a five-width satin stitch (Fig. 1.3; see Texturing Techniques Box) and sew, centering the design lines under your presser foot. Pull threads to the back and tie them off or use the lock-off function on your sewing machine. Remove the stabilizer by cutting or tearing it away.

3. Lay the garment or fabric on a flat surface protected with layers of paper towel. Squirt a bead of Fiber-Etch along the inside of the satin-stitched edge. On heavier fabrics such as denim, you may have to treat the back of the fabric as well. Let the gel dry overnight or use a hair dryer if you are in a hurry (Fig. 1.4).

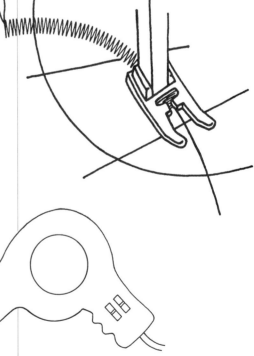

Fig. 1.3: *Sew, centering wide satin stitches over design lines.*

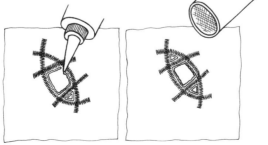

Fig. 1.4:
Squirt a bead of the fabric remover gel along the inside edge of the stitches. Dry fabric overnight or with a hair dryer.

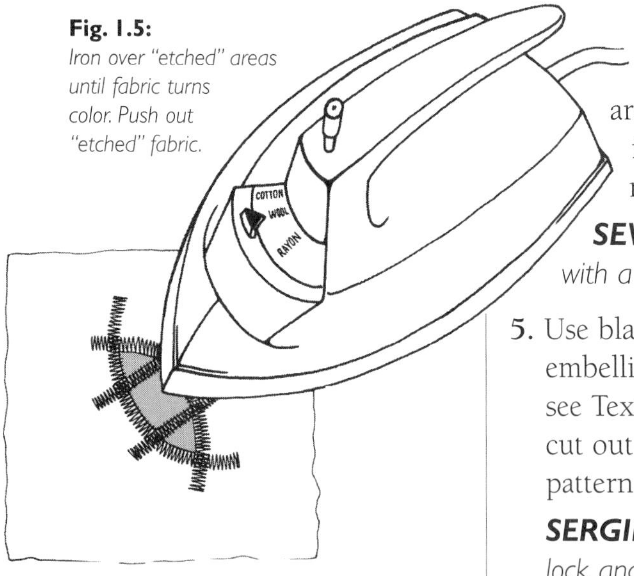

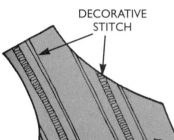

Fig. 1.5:
Iron over "etched" areas until fabric turns color. Push out "etched" fabric.

4. Set your iron on wool. Press over the "etched" area (Fig. 1.5). After several seconds, remove the iron (the area should turn a darker color or brown) and test by poking your finger into the etched fabric. Remove fabric if it's ready, or press again (see product instructions).

SEW-HOW: *If the etched edge shows fabric color, brush over it with a permanent marker that matches the thread.*

5. Use black machine embroidery thread and a decorative stitch to embellish narrow stripes on both sides of the cutwork (Fig. 1.6; see Texturing Techniques Box). If you are constructing the vest, cut out fronts and back, then sew or serge together following the pattern guide sheet.

SERGING SAVVY: *Texture a stripe using the ladder side of the flatlock and black thread (Fig. 1.7; see Texturing Techniques Box).*

6. Using the button sewing foot, replace the buttons that came on the vest with more interesting ones, then add additional texture by sewing buttons on other stripes (see Texturing Techniques Box).

VARIATIONS: *Fiber-Etch won't burn away painted edges, so you can create your design using fabric paints instead of satin stitches for a no-sew alternative. Use Fiber-Etch "cutwork" on collars, cuffs, bibs, yokes, or pockets. For more interest, use fabrics that are a blend of natural and synthetic fibers. The natural fiber (except silk) will burn away, leaving the synthetic fiber showing for a sheer, tone-on-tone effect (Fig. 1.8). Or try satin stitching over a printed design, then cut or burn away the inside. The possibilities are almost endless.*

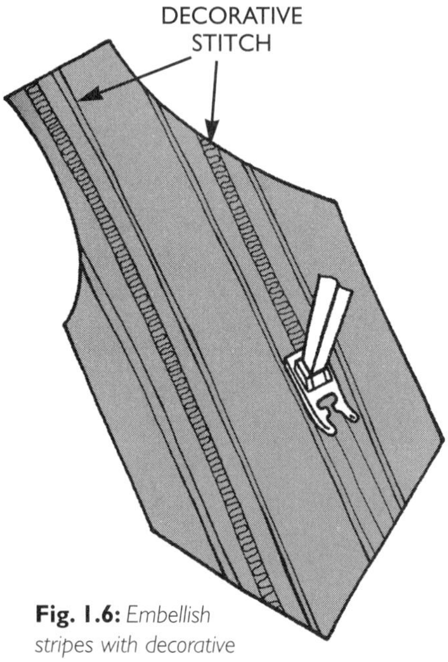

DECORATIVE
STITCH

Fig. 1.6: *Embellish stripes with decorative stitching and a contrasting thread.*

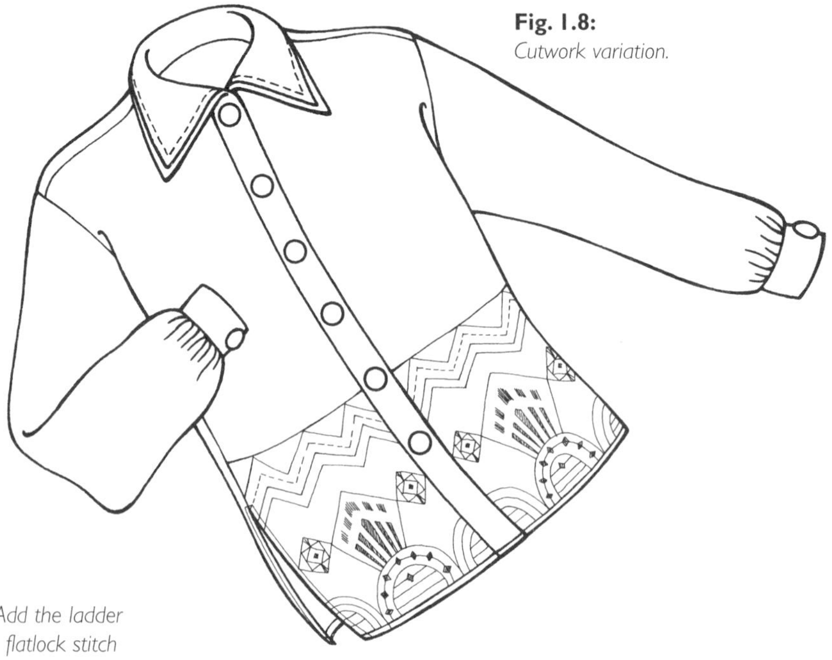

FLATLOCKING
LADDERS

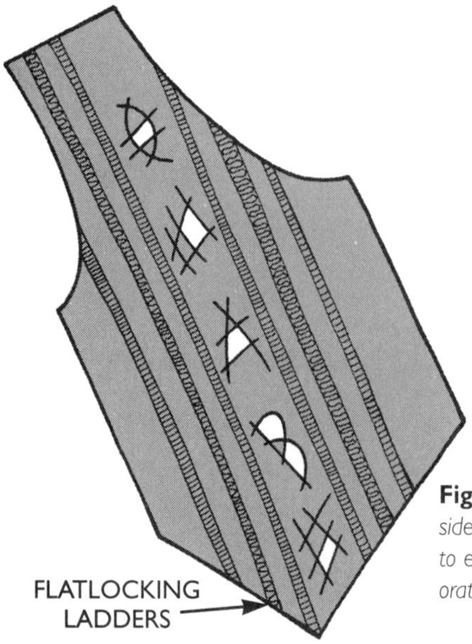

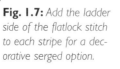

Fig. 1.7: *Add the ladder side of the flatlock stitch to each stripe for a decorative serged option.*

Fig. 1.8:
Cutwork variation.

PETROGLYPH PETS

Petroglyphs (primitive carvings or line-drawings on rock) have always intrigued us. When we planned an allover design, we were inspired to use easy-to-stitch geometric shapes. We added color by using reverse appliqué — the process of slipping colorful appliqués under a shirt fabric (rather than attaching them on top of the shirt), stitching them in place, then removing the shirt fabric over the appliqué to reveal the fabric underneath.

TEXTURING TECHNIQUES

(SEW) **Transferring Designs with Ease** . . . . p. 77

🧵 **Reverse Appliqué**

🧵 **Satin and Decorative Stitch Strategy** . . . . . p. 74

🧵 **Couching the Carefree Way (optional)** . . . . . p. 63

🧵 **Making Wide Serger Braid (optional)** . . p. 64

You'll Need:

Fabric
- One starched denim or chambray shirt
- Sixteen colorful scraps for appliqués (one 2" [5cm] square per pet)

Needle
- 90/14 jeans

Thread
- *Top:* machine embroidery thread in the same colors as fabric scraps
- *Bobbin:* blue machine embroidery thread a shade darker than shirt

Presser Foot
- Embroidery/appliqué

Stabilizer
- Tear-away

Miscellaneous
- Disappearing marker
- Tracing or typing paper
- Appliqué or sharp embroidery scissors
- Dressmaker's carbon and empty ballpoint pen or heat-transfer pen
- Serger braid (optional; see Texturing Techniques Box)
- Scissors
- Pins

Fig. I.9: *Petroglyph Pets.*

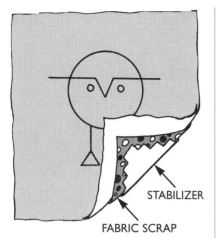

Fig. 1.10: *Layer fabric scrap over stabilizer and slip under each pet so scrap is sandwiched between the shirt and stabilizer, and so the right side of the scrap is against the wrong side of the shirt..*

Fig. 1.11: *After stitching, carefully trim away the top fabric to allow the bottom fabric to peek through.*

Fig. 1.12: *Beaks taper out to a five-width satin stitch; legs are a two-width satin stitch, and feet are stitched freely to create triangles.*

To Texture:

1. Use a copy machine to make five copies of the Petroglyph Pet designs found at the end of this chapter. Cut pets apart, trimming close to the designs. Arrange pets on shirt back (we put six pets on the back and ten on the front). Place dressmaker's carbon under each paper pet, then transfer by tracing over paper pets with an empty ballpoint pen (see Texturing Techniques Box). Repeat for shirt front. Use the disappearing marker and draw over the carbon lines.

SEW-HOW: *A quick way to transfer designs used several times is with a heat-transfer pen (see Texturing Techniques Box). We used the Sulky Iron-on Transfer Pen with good results.*

2. Pin colorful scraps over the pets to check for a pleasant overall effect. Once satisfied, place each fabric scrap face up on a larger scrap of stabilizer and slip the two pieces under the appropriate pet shape. The fabric scrap will be sandwiched between the shirt and the stabilizer, and the right side of the fabric scrap is against the wrong side of the shirt (Fig. 1.10). Using thread that matches the scrap, outline each shape with a straight stitch. *Note:* Use the same color thread for this straight stitch as you plan to use for satin stitching the shapes.

3. Use your embroidery or appliqué scissors and carefully trim away the denim or chambray from the inside of each pet body, leaving the scrap fabric to show through the hole (Fig. 1.11). Satin-stitch over the straight stitch lines using a two-width zigzag (see Texturing Techniques Box). Lock or tie off stitches at the beginning and end of each shape.

4. Go back and fill in the other parts of the designs. Some beaks are five-width satin-stitched triangles (these and similar motifs are built into some machines). Use a wide zigzag stitch and stitch in one place several times to create blobs for eyes; legs are a two-width satin stitch; feet are stitched in freely after outlining to create the triangles (Fig. 1.12). Turn the shirt inside out, remove the stabilizer, and trim back the scraps almost to the stitching.

5. Place shirt on a flat surface. Starting at the bottom front and traveling up over the closest shoulder, down the back, up over the other shoulder, and down the other front, draw a winding path from one pet to the next. Sew a decorative stitch that looks like footprints (we used the feather stitch; see Texturing Techniques Box), or couch light-colored serger braid over your marked lines (see Texturing Techniques Box). This should be an understated path; the pets should be the most prominent part of the design.

PRESSING MATTERS: *If the shirt has softened up, spray-starch and press it before stitching the path.*

6. Use one of the embroidery threads to topstitch over the pockets, collar, cuff, and placket. This pulls everything together into one terrific top.

VARIATIONS: *Instead of satin-stitching over the straight stitches, use fabric paint. Use synthetic fabric scraps to back the reverse appliqué, then spread Fiber-Etch on each pet body to dissolve the cotton denim or chambray.*

PEEK-A-BUTTON VEST

Capture buttons in a see-through crazy-quilt vest. Here it tops a dress, so the fabric used for the bias binding is the same as the dress fabric. The buttons match the colors found in the print. Of course, you can buy commercial bias tape to save a step.

Fig. 1.13:
Peek-A-Button Vest.

> ## TEXTURING TECHNIQUES
>
> 🧵 **Straight-Stitching See-Through Pockets**
>
> 🧵 **Decorative Stitch Strategy** . . . p. 74
>
> 🧵 OR 🧵 **Bias Tape Application**

You'll Need:

Fabric

- 1 package of ¹/₂" (1.3cm) bias tape or scraps of dress fabric cut into 2" (5cm) bias strips (enough to make about 2-¹/₂ yards (2.5m)
- Can-Can net (a 54"- [137cm] wide nylon netting that's softer than kitchen-scrubber netting and stiffer than bridal tulle)

Needle

- 80/12 universal

Thread

- Monofilament for pocket construction
- Variegated machine-embroidery cotton thread for decorative stitching
- All-purpose thread for vest construction

Presser Feet

- Standard
- Embroidery

Miscellaneous

- Vest pattern (no side seams preferred)
- 6 dozen buttons in assorted sizes and colors
- ¹/₂" (1.3cm) bias tape maker

To Texture:

1. Using a commercial pattern, cut two layers of Can-Can net for the vest. Round off any vest corners for ease in construction later.

2. Pin the layers together, then sew around the edges using all-purpose thread and leaving an opening in one place large enough to

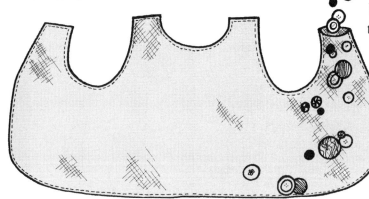

Fig. 1.14:
*Stitch around all vest edges, leaving an
opening to pour in the buttons.*

insert all the button sizes. Pour in the buttons, then stitch the opening closed (Fig. 1.14).

3. Starting with the front shoulder, move a button to the top and use monofilament thread to straight stitch a line underneath the button from the neck edge to the armhole, trapping the button inside. Continue in this manner until all the buttons are caught in see-through pockets (Fig. 1.15).*Optional:* Skip this step and go directly to step four, using the decorative stitching to create the pockets.

SEW-HOW: *Enclose several buttons in a large space, then go back and stitch off smaller areas in that space, slipping one of the buttons in each space as you go. Vary the shape of these spaces for eye-appeal.*

SHOULDER

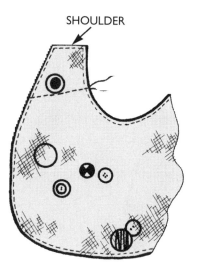

Fig. 1.15: *Trap a button in a section by sewing from one side of the stitching to the other.*

4. Now choose the decorative machine stitch you'll use. Change to the embroidery presser foot and use machine embroidery thread to stitch over the straight stitches defining each pocket. (We chose the feather stitch and used yellow/white variegated thread for interest.) Remember to lock stitches before and after a line of stitching by using your lock-off function or stitching back and forth with the stitch length at 0.

5. Sew or serge the shoulder seams together using a 1/4" (6mm) seam finish. Press seam allowances toward the front, then top-stitch over the seams using the same decorative stitch as before.

6. If you have purchased bias tape, skip this step. To make bias tape, use a bias tape maker. This is a sewing notion that folds the fabric edges to the middle as you pull the fabric through. Then, simply press down the folds with a steam iron as the strip emerges from the tape maker (Fig. 1.16).

Fig. 1.16: *Make bias tape by pressing the folds as the fabric comes out of the cone of the bias tape maker.*

7. Rethread your machine with all-purpose thread. Open one edge of the bias tape and place the right side of the bias tape against the wrong side of the vest so the raw edges are even. Sew a line of straight stitches in the fold to attach the bias tape to the vest (Fig. 1.17) or use the serger to attach the tape. Wrap the bias around the edge, bringing it to the front side of the vest. Topstitch using the sewing machine and the same decorative thread and stitch you used in step four (Fig. 1.18).

VARIATIONS: *Use a finer net or other sheer fabric and fill pockets with charms, semi-precious stones, appliqués, laces, or flat beads available in craft stores.*

Now that you have a taste of fabric texturing, discover the possibilities when we add Simple Surface Transformations — Textures Applied Flat to the Fabric in Chapter Two.

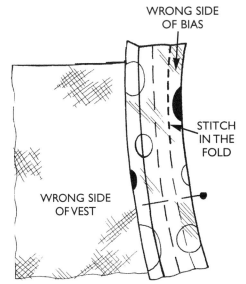

Fig. 1.17: *Open one edge of the bias tape and place the right side of the bias tape against the wrong side of the vest so the raw edges are even. Sew a line of straight stitches in the fold to attach the bias tape to the vest.*

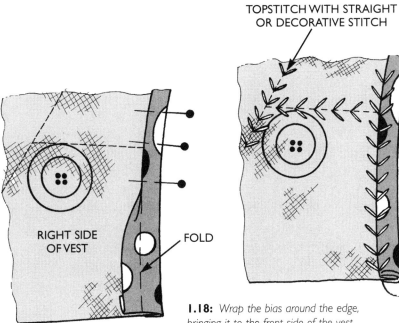

1.18: *Wrap the bias around the edge, bringing it to the front side of the vest. Topstitch using the same decorative thread and stitch as before.*

ZIPPY DOODLE DESIGNS

Chapter 1 Patterns

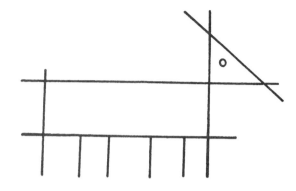

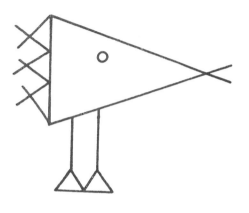

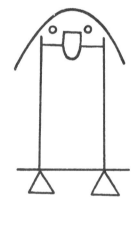

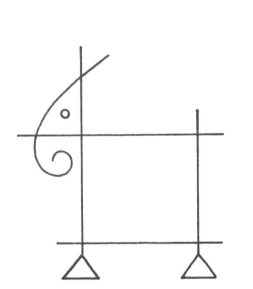

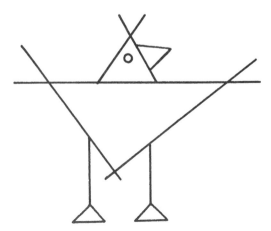

PETROGLYPH PETS DESIGNS

Doodle Page

POSSIBLE TEXTURING PROJECTS

Garment I'd Like to Texture	Technique	Page#	Sketch of Project
1.			
2.			
3.			
4.			
5.			

Chapter 2

SIMPLE SURFACE TRANSFORMATIONS

Textures Applied Flat to the Fabric

In the past, the term "surface texture" often meant appliqué. But that's only a hint of the possibilities. We hope the techniques in this chapter expand your creative horizons.

BREAKING THE BOUNDARIES

We often have boundaries—like coloring in the lines. How confining! Even though we'd gone so far as decorating the yoke edges with decorative machine stitches, we broke through those stitched boundaries to add satin-stitched bars over the front and down the back asymmetrically, making the design take on a life of its own.

Fig. 2.1: *Breaking The Boundaries.*

> ## TEXTURING TECHNIQUES
>
> 🧵 **Decorative Stitch Strategy** . . . p. 74
>
> 🧵 **Satin-Stitched Bars, Blobs, and Circles** . . . . p. 74
>
> 🧵 **Couching the Carefree Way** . . . p. 63
>
> 🧵 **Making Wide Serger Braid (optional)** . . . . p. 64

You'll Need:

Fabric
- Pre-shrunk starched ready-made garment to decorate

Needle
- 90/14 jeans

Thread
- *Top:* rayon machine embroidery thread (we used red, yellow, green, blue, orange, and purple)
- *Bobbin:* darning thread

Presser Foot
- Embroidery/appliqué

Stabilizer
- Tear-away or iron-on tear-away

Miscellaneous
- Disappearing marker or disappearing chalk
- Serger braid (see Texturing Techniques Box)

To Texture:

1. After testing on a denim or chambray scrap, use your decorative machine stitches to decorate around collar, yoke, and front placket (see Texturing Techniques Box). Use red thread on the collar and one side of the placket; use blue around the yoke and the other side of the placket. Also decorate around the cuffs with red or blue stitching. We found that filled-in satin-type stitches used on the widest width gave the best effect.

2. Draw bars freely on yoke and down the shirt back with the disappearing marker or chalk, using the Breaking the Boundaries design at the end of the chapter as a guide. Place iron-on stabilizer under bars, slightly loosen the upper tension, then use a five-

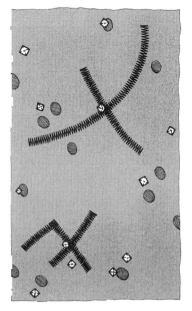

Fig. 2.2: *Add satin stitched circles and blobs; add rhinestones, or studs for even more texture.*

to six-width satin stitch to make each one (see Texturing Techniques Box). Remember to anchor them at the beginning and end of each bar by using your machine's lock-off function or by stitching in place.

SERGING SAVVY: *For a more textured effect, replace the wide satin-stitched bars with serger braid you've made and couched to the shirt (see Texturing Techniques Box).*

3. Add stitched confetti (individual round or football-shaped motifs made using satin stitches).

VARIATIONS: *Add even more texture by attaching studs or rhinestones (following manufacturer's instructions) or dot paint blobs around the bars to make more confetti (Fig. 2.2).*

SCRAP HAPPY

Talk about recycling. This embellished shirt is made completely from scraps we found on the sewing room floor. Fabric pieces no larger than 2" (5cm) are stitched down with Sliver or Stream Lamé metallic variegated thread to create new fabric.

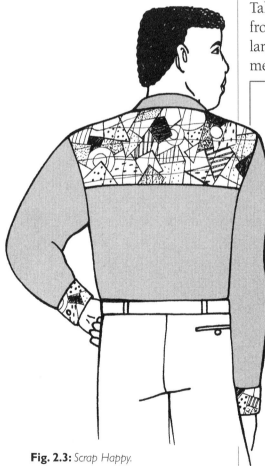

Fig. 2.3: *Scrap Happy.*

TEXTURING TECHNIQUES	
🧵 **Free-Machine Embroidery**	. . . p. 67
🧵 **Couching the Carefree Way**	. . p. 63
🧵 **Satin Stitch Strategy**	. . . . p. 74
🧵 **"Satin Serging" a Narrow Rolled Edge**	. . . . p. 76

You'll Need:

Fabric
- Pre-shrunk starched ready-made garment to decorate; pre-shrunk scraps no larger than 2" (5cm) square each — enough to cover area of yoke, cuffs, and pocket flaps (approximately 18" (46cm) square)

Needle
- 90/14 jeans or embroidery

Thread
- *Top:* flat Sliver, Tinsel Stream Lamé variegated metallic thread, rayon machine embroidery thread, or Prizm
- *Bobbin:* darning embroidery or all-purpose sewing thread
- *Serger needle:* all-purpose serger thread
- *Upper looper:* Woolly Nylon or rayon embroidery thread
- *Lower looper:* all-purpose serger thread

Presser Feet
- Darning, embroidery/appliqué, cording or braiding

Miscellaneous
- Glue stick
- Red #5 pearl cotton
- Pinking or wave rotary cutter and mat

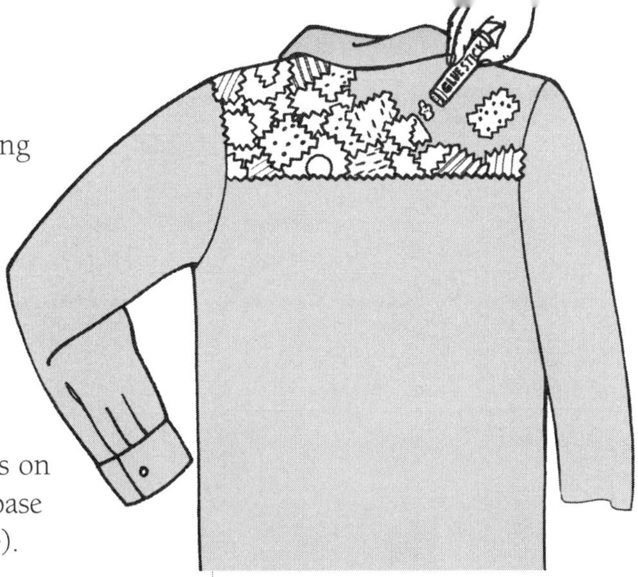

To Texture:

1. Gather your scraps from previous projects. Cut up scraps using the pinking or wave rotary cutter, and dot scrap backs with your glue stick. Arrange scraps on back yoke, overlapping edges. If you want, let the base fabric show through the scraps for interest (Fig. 2.4).

2. Prepare for free-machine stitching by lowering or covering the feed dogs and attaching the darning foot to your sewing machine (see Texturing Techniques Box). Using the flat metallic thread, straight stitch freely up and back, stitching in an elongated zigzag motion (Fig. 2.5). If you want to create a more dense effect, make your first "zigzags" 1" (2.5cm) long, then drop down at least 2" (5cm), and proceed again, creating another row of 1" (2.5cm) "zigzags." Continue until you have covered the piece of fabric.

3. Turn the fabric 90 degrees and stitch in the same manner in the other direction.

4. Repeat steps one, two, and three for cuffs. No need to remove buttons, just stitch carefully around them. You can even stitch over the buttonholes, then cut through and freely straight stitch around them to reinforce the holes. If your shirt has flaps, you may want to remove them, and repeat steps one, two, and three.

5. Bring your feed dogs up or uncover them and put your braiding or cording foot on. Change top thread to red rayon embroidery. Using a two-length (13 stitches per inch) and two-width zigzag, couch red pearl cotton around the edges of the yoke, cuffs, and pocket flaps. Cut cord ends off at the fabric, then go back and satin stitch over cord for a beautiful finish (Fig. 2.6; see Texturing Techniques Box).

SERGING SAVVY: *Rather than satin stitching, remove the pocket flap, set your serger for a narrow rolled edge using rayon embroidery thread in the upper looper; then serge around the edges of the pocket. Reattach flap by stitching-in-the-ditch along the top edge (Fig. 2.7).*

VARIATIONS: *Try this collage technique to create textured yardage and use your "new fabric" to make a tote bag, cosmetic bag, or a pocket.*

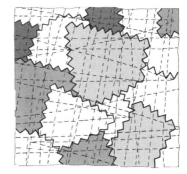

Fig. 2.4: *Arrange scraps on back yoke, overlapping edges so the base fabric shows through the squares.*

Fig. 2.5: *Using flat metallic thread in the needle, freely straight stitch over squares going up and back in an elongated zigzag pattern.*

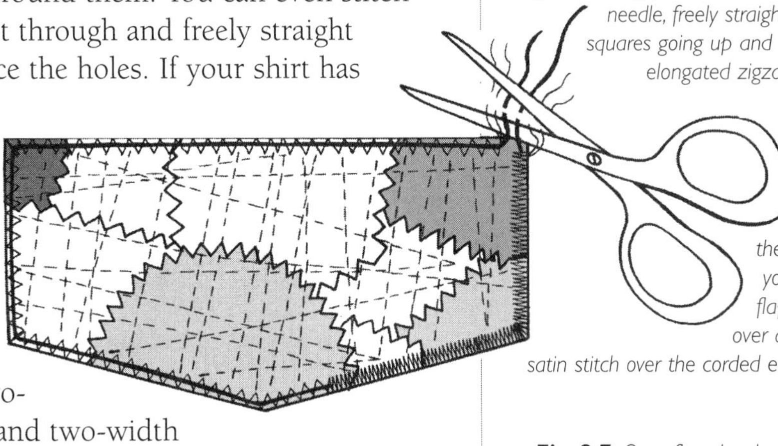

Fig. 2.6: *Decorate the edge of the yoke, cuff, or flap by couching over a cord. Then satin stitch over the corded edge.*

Fig. 2.7: *On a flap that has been serged with a narrow rolled edge, stitch-in-the-ditch next to the edge to attach flap to shirt.*

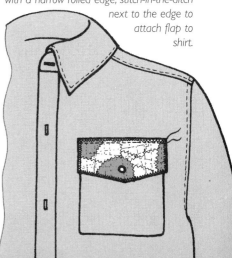

Simple Surface Transformations **19**

SCRAP-SAVER'S REMOVABLE YOKE

Make removable yokes, collars, and cuffs for a favorite button-down sweater, pullover, or sweatshirt.

Fig. 2.8: *Scrap-Saver's Removable Yoke.*

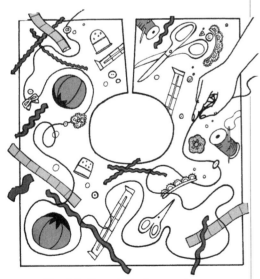

Fig. 2.9: *Place appliqués over yoke foundation, then sprinkle sequins and other goodies over the rest of the yoke in a pleasing arrangement.*

TEXTURING TECHNIQUES

- (SEW) **Creating a Garment-Part Pattern** . . . . p. 77
- **Sheer-Overlay Appliqué**
- **Free-Machine Embroidery** . . . p. 67
- **Making Narrow Serger Cord** . . . . p. 65
- **Serge-Wrapped Corners (optional)**
- **"Satin Serging" Strategy (for neck edges)** . . . . p. 75

You'll Need:

Fabric

- ½ yard (0.45m) pre-shrunk fabric printed with sewing notions, scissors, and thread (these will be cut out and used as appliqués)
- ½ yard (0.45m) contrasting fabric for lining
- ¼ yard (0.2m) navy bridal tulle
- ½ yard (0.45m) pre-shrunk allover sewing print for the foundation (we used a fabric from Fabric Traditions)

Needle

- 90/14 stretch or embroidery

Thread

- *Top:* monofilament   • *Bobbin:* monofilament
- *Serger needle:* coordinating all-purpose serger thread
- *Upper looper:* #5 pearl cotton or other decorative cord
- *Lower looper:* coordinating all-purpose serger thread

Presser Feet

- Darning or darning spring   • Standard zigzag
- Edge-stitch   • Button sewing

Stabilizer

- Tear-away

Miscellaneous

- Sequins   • Pins
- Five standard flat buttons   • Hot glue and glue gun
- Double-eyed or tapestry needle

- Plastic or printed ribbon tape measure
- Narrow serger cord (see Texturing Techniques Box)
- Rickrack, bits and pieces of trims you have on hand
- Five ceramic buttons and button cover forms

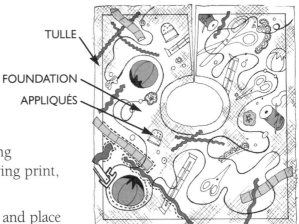

TULLE

FOUNDATION

APPLIQUÉS

To Texture:

1. Trace the yoke from any ready-made shirt (see Texturing Techniques Box). Cut one yoke each of the allover sewing print, bridal tulle, and lining fabric.

2. From the large printed fabric, cut out sewing appliqués, and place them on the allover-print yoke foundation, using a glue stick to keep the appliqués from shifting. Sprinkle sequins, tape-measure pieces, cord, rickrack, narrow serger cord, thread chains, and other bits and pieces over the appliqués and foundation (Fig. 2.9).

3. Lay navy tulle (or tulle the color of your background fabric) over the yoke foundation, pinning it in place so things don't move. Place the tear-away stabilizer under the yoke.

4. Set your machine for free-machine embroidery (see Texturing Techniques Box), and stitch around the appliqués, capturing them in the tulle so the raw edges won't fray. Continue freely stitching over remaining foundation between the appliqués and other elements to hold everything in place (Fig. 2.10; see Texturing Techniques Box).

5. Sew or serge the yoke together leaving the neck open to turn it through. Turn the yoke right side out, press it, and edge-stitch all the straight edges.

   SERGING SAVVY: *For a great-looking yoke that doesn't have to be edge-stitched and that lies flat and smooth, serge it together with right sides together and wrap the corners as you go (Fig. 2.11).*

6. Using the pearl cotton or other decorative thread in the upper looper, serge around the neck edge using a short satin-stitch length and a balanced three-thread overlock (see Texturing Techniques Box). Serge at least a 3" (7.5cm) chain on one side to make a button loop. Pull loose threads back under the stitching on the other side of neck opening (Fig. 2.12). Sew on button, and hand or machine tack the serged chain to make a loop that fits the button.

   VARIATIONS: *Make removable collars or decorate children's clothing using hobby or special interest themes such as fishing, sailing, gardening, or favorite cartoon characters. Start with sneaker fabric for runners, nursery fabrics for new mothers or day-care teachers, and then, instead of overlaying the fabric and keepsakes with tulle, cover, fuse, and laminate your textures to hold them in place. Then cut the laminated fabric up to make almost-no-sew book covers, tote bags, eyeglass cases and other fashion accessories — the possibilities are practically endless.*

Fig. 2.10: *After pinning the tulle over the yoke, free-machine embroider around the appliqués, capturing them between the tulle and yoke foundation.*

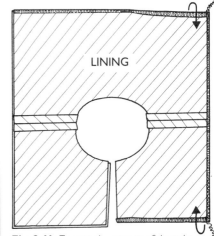

LINING

Fig. 2.11: *To wrap the corners of the yoke, put lining and yoke pieces right sides together. Serge along the front edge and the two flap edges opposite it. With the lining side up, fold these edges toward the center of the yoke and serge along the other straight edges of the yoke, catching the end folds in the serging.*

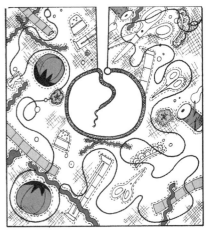

Fig. 2.12: *Using pearl cotton or other decorative cord in the upper looper, serge around neck edge with a satin stitch. Chain off one end so you have enough serged cord to make a button loop.*

WARP-AND-WOOF WEAR

In weaving vernacular, the warp and woof are the crosswise and lengthwise fibers used to weave a piece of fabric in a loom. In this quick-to-make texturing treatment, we weave strips of fabric, then add buttons and cords to texture this yoke — a great way to use some favorite fabrics when you don't have enough for a whole project.

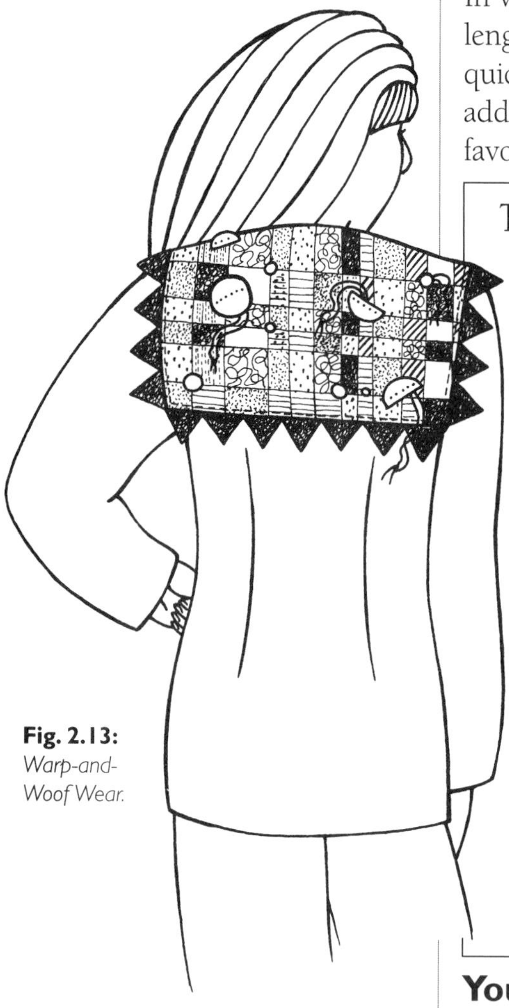

Fig. 2.13:
Warp-and-Woof Wear.

TEXTURING TECHNIQUES

SEW	**Creating a Garment-Part Pattern**	. . . . . . p. 77
SEW	**Fabric Weaving**	
	Quick-Cut Fringe Points	
	Free-Machine Embroidery and Granite Stitching	. . . . p. 67
	Button Sewing — But Not by Hand	. . . . p. 62
OR	**Piping Up for Texture**	. . . . . . p. 70
OR	**Fabric Tubes Made Fast and Fun (optional)**	. . . . . p. 65
	"Satin Serging" a Narrow Rolled Edge	. . . . p. 76

You'll Need:

Fabric
- Pre-shrunk starched ready-made garment to decorate
- Different widths/colors of light and dark print fabrics (totaling approximately ⅝ yard [0.5m] square)
- Red denim, broadcloth, or cotton gabardine 6" × 30" (15cm × 76cm)

Needle
- 90/14 jeans

Thread
- *Top:* cotton or rayon machine embroidery thread; all-purpose sewing thread
- *Bobbin:* monofilament, darning, or all-purpose thread
- *Serger needle:* all-purpose serger thread
- *Upper looper:* Woolly Nylon or rayon thread
- *Lower looper:* all-purpose serger thread

Presser Feet
- Embroidery/appliqué
- Darning

Stabilizer

- 14" × 22" (35.3cm × 56cm) piece of paper-backed fusible web

Miscellaneous

- Rotary cutter and board
- Clear plastic ruler
- Disappearing marker
- Three dozen assorted red buttons
- Yoke pattern (see Texturing Techniques Box)
- Several yards (meters) of red #5 pearl cotton

To Texture:

1. Make a yoke pattern from a ready-made shirt (see Texturing Techniques Box) and add 1/4" (6mm) seam allowance. Draw yoke outline on the web side of paper-backed fusible web using the disappearing marker, but don't cut it out yet.

2. Cut out fabric strips of varying widths but no wider than 1-1/4" (3cm) and at least 22" (56cm) long. (*Optional:* With your serger, narrow roll the edges of several strips, leaving the remainder with raw edges [see Texturing Techniques Box]).

3. To weave strips, place the long ones horizontally on the web side of the yoke pattern. Pin through to the paper. Alternate dark and light strips for best results. Starting in the middle, weave perpendicular strips from the center out, cutting strips to length only after you are satisfied with how it looks (Fig. 2.14). The woven strips should cover the yoke pattern. Press strips to fusible web; cool, then remove pins and paper. Cut out yoke and either turn back the seam allowances and press them, add piping (see Texturing Techniques Box), or serge-finish the yoke edges with a balanced, decorative three-thread serged satin stitch around all four sides (see Texturing Techniques Box).

4. To make the quick-cut fringe points, fold the 30" (76cm) red fabric strip in half the long way. Fuse wrong sides together using paper-backed fusible web and following manufacturer's instructions. Using the disappearing marker, draw fringe points that are 2-1/2" (16.5cm) deep and 2" (5cm) wide and leave a 1/2" (1.3cm) seam allowance along each edge. Stitch on both sides of the drawn line, leaving enough room between the two rows of stitching to cut the points apart (Fig. 2.15).

5. Beginning at the center back of the shirt's yoke, pin the straight edge of the fringe points to the back, sides, and front edges of the shirt's yoke, placing the fringe's 1/2" (5cm) seam allowance just

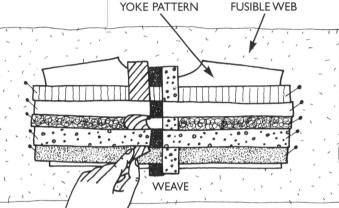

YOKE PATTERN   FUSIBLE WEB

WEAVE

Fig. 2.14: *Draw yoke pattern on the web side of paper-backed fusible web. Weave cut and serged-edge strips over web from the middle out, pinning strips on either end as you go.*

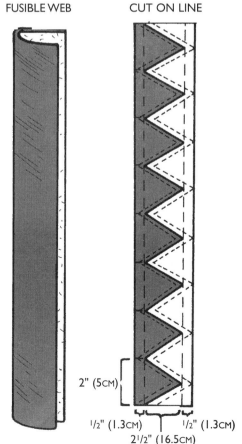

FUSIBLE WEB   CUT ON LINE

2" (5CM)

1/2" (1.3CM)   1/2" (1.3CM)

2 1/2" (16.5CM)

Fig. 2.15: *Fold and fuse red strip in half the long way. Mark the quick-cut fringe points, cutting the strip apart on the drawn line. Remember to leave 1/2" (1.3cm) seam allowances on both edges.*

inside the yoke edge. Position the woven yoke, right side up, over the shirt's yoke and stitch it down along the top edge of the points using monofilament thread. Add two points to the pocket top. (*Optional:* If the points become too wild-looking, stitch them to the shirt, sewing along the original stitching on the points.)

6. For additional texture, set your machine for free-machine embroidery, using red machine embroidery thread through the needle (see Texturing Techniques Box). Then freely stitch over weaving in a granite stitch pattern. Replace shirt buttons with red ones and machine stitch them on (see Texturing Techniques Box). Hand-stitch larger buttons to yoke using red pearl cotton, letting the cord ends hang down 3" (7.5cm), then machine-stitch smaller buttons adding more texture to the yoke.

VARIATIONS: *Weave tubes or ribbons and use the same idea for pockets, pillows, and handbags. Weave jacket or vest lapels using fabric strips with cross-locked beads or trim. Use the quick-cut fringe points to edge pillows, hems of full skirts, quilt edges, and duvet covers (Fig. 2.16).*

Fig. 2.16:
Warp-and-Woof Wear variations.

SLAP-DASH AND PATCH

There weren't *that* many holes in this shirt, but we slapped on the patches so no one can tell which one or two are the authentic "hole covers." We think this fix-it-up texturing technique is good-looking enough to do on a shirt without the holes, don't you?

TEXTURING TECHNIQUES

Fig. 2.17:
Slap-Dash and Patch.

You'll Need:

Fabric

- Pre-shrunk starched ready-made garment to decorate
- 1/8–1/4 yard (0.2–0.4m) pre-shrunk coordinating woven cotton prints (we used a red, white, blue, and green color scheme)

Needle

- 90/14 jeans

Thread

- *Top:* color-coordinating cotton or rayon embroidery thread; monofilament
- *Bobbin:* all-purpose sewing thread; monofilament
- *Serger needle:* blue all-purpose serger thread
- *Upper looper:* variegated #8 pearl cotton
- *Lower looper:* all-purpose serger thread

Presser Feet

- Button sewing
- Embroidery/appliqué
- Cording or braiding

Stabilizer

- Tear-away

Miscellaneous

- 1/2 yard (0.45m) paper-backed fusible web
- Rotary cutter and board
- Dozen each of red, green, and blue assorted-sized buttons
- Three yards (2.8m) jumbo rickrack

To Texture:

1. Back cotton prints with paper-backed fusible web and cut into squares, rectangles, and triangles; then arrange on shirt front and back.

   SERGING SAVVY: *If you want your patches to be softer, finish around them using either a narrow rolled edge (see Texturing Techniques Box) or a balanced three-thread serged satin stitch using fusible thread in the lower looper (see Texturing Techniques Box). Fuse patches; then topstitch or edge-stitch them in place.*

2. Using wide satin stitches, stitch around each appliqué using contrasting thread (see Texturing Techniques Box). If you don't use the shirt pockets, don't hesitate to place patches over them, too. Accent satin stitches by stitching next to or on top of them with decorative machine stitches and contrasting thread (Fig. 2.18; see Texturing Techniques Box).

3. Make narrow serger braid (see Texturing Techniques Box) and couch it down randomly to tie all the patches together (see Texturing Techniques Box). Use monofilament thread top and bobbin, your cording or narrow braiding foot, and a two-length (13 stitches per inch), three-width zigzag stitch.

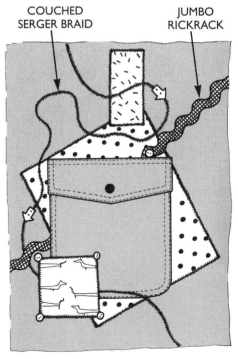

COUCHED SERGER BRAID

JUMBO RICKRACK

Fig. 2.18: *Satin stitched patches accented with decorative machine stitches, narrow serged cord, buttons, and rickrack.*

4. Stitch down the center of the jumbo rickrack with a straight stitch or open zigzag and monofilament thread. Now add a decorative touch with buttons of all sizes, stitching them in place with the button sewing foot and contrasting machine embroidery thread through the needle (see Texturing Techniques Box). Remove shirt closure buttons and replace them with colorful buttons to match the shirt decoration.

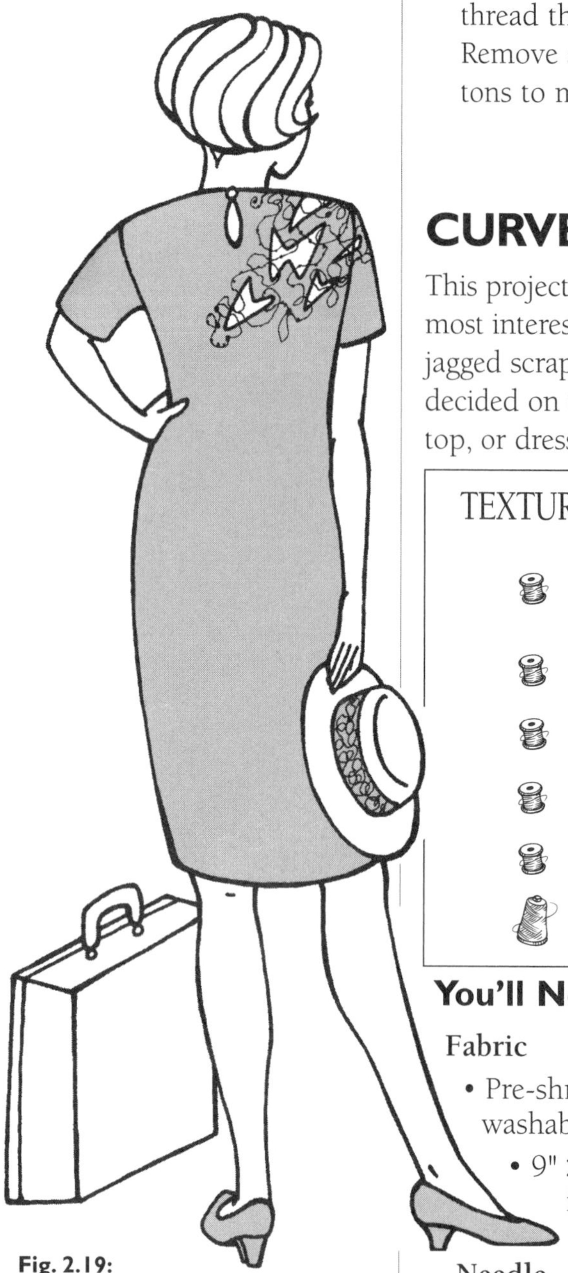

CURVES AND CORNERS

This project proves that sometimes the simplest designs produce the most interesting results. Call them streaks of lightening, zigzags, or jagged scraps. We began with two different appliqué designs. Once we decided on the fabric, the rest was easy. We ended up with a shirt, top, or dress even a grandmother can love and wear — Jackie does.

Fig. 2.19:
Curves and Corners.

TEXTURING TECHNIQUES

Appliqué with Turned-Back Edges . . . . p. 56

Couching the Carefree Way . . . p. 63

Satin-Stitched "Blobs" . . . . p. 74

Free-Machine Embroidery . . . p. 67

Beads, Baubles, and Bangles . . . p. 59

Making Narrow Serger Braid . . p. 64

You'll Need:

Fabric
- Pre-shrunk starched ready-made woven shirt or chemise in a washable fabric
  - 9" × 18" (23cm × 46cm) colorful woven and printed square fabric (ours included red, orange, royal blue, purple, gold, and peach)

Needle
- 90/14 jeans or embroidery
- 65/9 universal

Thread
- *Top:* color-coordinating cotton embroidery thread, Sliver, Tinsel Stream Lamé, or Prizm in gold
- *Bobbin:* all-purpose sewing thread
- *Serger needle and lower looper:* gold metallic thread
- *Upper looper:* gold metallic ribbon floss

Presser Feet
- Standard zigzag
- Darning
- Embroidery/appliqué
- Pearls and piping

Stabilizer
- Iron-on tear-away
- Water-soluble for appliqué

Miscellaneous
- Glue stick
- Disappearing marker
- Teflon pressing sheet
- Gold beads and baubles
- Color-coordinating seed beads
- Beading hand needle (optional)
- 2 yards (1.85 m) cross-locked beads
- Lavender metallic ribbon floss for filler cord of serger braid
- Brass watch cogs (available at your local craft store)

To Texture:

1. Photocopy or trace four copies of Curves and Corners designs at the end of this chapter. Arrange the patterns over the garment until you are pleased with the look — we placed seven on the yoke and across the shoulders and one on the right cuff.

2. Make appliqués with turned-back edges (see Texturing Techniques Box). Glue-stick the appliqués in place on the project. Thread your needle with Sliver or Tinsel Stream Lamé and blanket stitch around each appliqué.

3. Make two yards of narrow serger braid, using a balanced narrow three-thread overlock serged over a filler cord of lavender metallic ribbon floss (see Texturing Techniques Box). Starting at the left side, place serged cord over appliqués, dotting glue stick on cord as you go along. Travel from the left side, draping cord over one shoulder, around the back, then over the other shoulder, and down the right sleeve. Place tear-away stabilizer underneath the path of the cord and under any other areas you plan to stitch (see steps four, five, and six).

4. Couch down serger cord with a two-length (13 stitches per inch), three-width zigzag (see Texturing Techniques Box).

5. Roughly following the serged cord placement, stitch purple satin-stitched blobs (see Texturing Techniques Box). To keep the threads between the blobs from snagging, go back and freely embroider between blobs as shown (Fig. 2.20; see Texturing Techniques Box).

6. Add single beads and baubles you've collected (see Texturing Techniques Box). Attach assorted gold disks with one hole in the center by hand. Jackie threaded a hand needle through the disk, a seed bead, and back down through the disk again.

7. Finish embellishment by couching cross-locked beads using the pearls and piping foot (see Texturing Techniques Box).

Go on to Chapter Three to see how to Transcend the Surface with Textures Raised Above the Fabric.

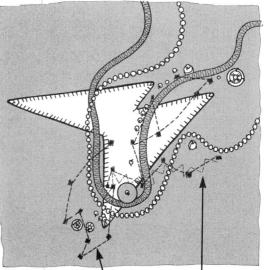

Fig. 2.20: *Add satin-stitch blobs, granite stitches, seed beads, brass disks, cross-locked beads, and narrow serged cord to Curves and Corners appliqués for a free-flowing texture.*

FREE MACHINE EMBROIDERY AND SATIN-STITCH BLOBS

EMBROIDERY BETWEEN SATIN-STITCH BLOBS

Chapter 2 Patterns

BREAKING THE
BOUNDARIES DESIGNS

CURVES AND CORNERS DESIGNS
(COPY OR TRACE FOUR)

Chapter 3

TRANSCENDING THE SURFACE

Textures Raised Above the Fabric

Use these ideas as a springboard for your own variations on dimensional textures. Use Easy-Angle Italian cording, Helter Skelter Serged Squares, It's-A-Miracle, or Flowering Denim techniques as a textural addition to solid fabric on a jacket or skirt.

THE EASY-ANGLE ITALIAN

Unlike traditional quilting, in which a layer of batting is sandwiched between two layers of fabric, Italian cording involves sandwiching a cord between two layers of fabric and sewing on either side of the cord to create a channel for the cord. Our stop-and-start version of this technique is easy to do, and the heavy thread used through the needle gives this texture a sashiko feeling. For additional texture, try threading beads over the yarn and leaving the yarn ends free to ravel or fray.

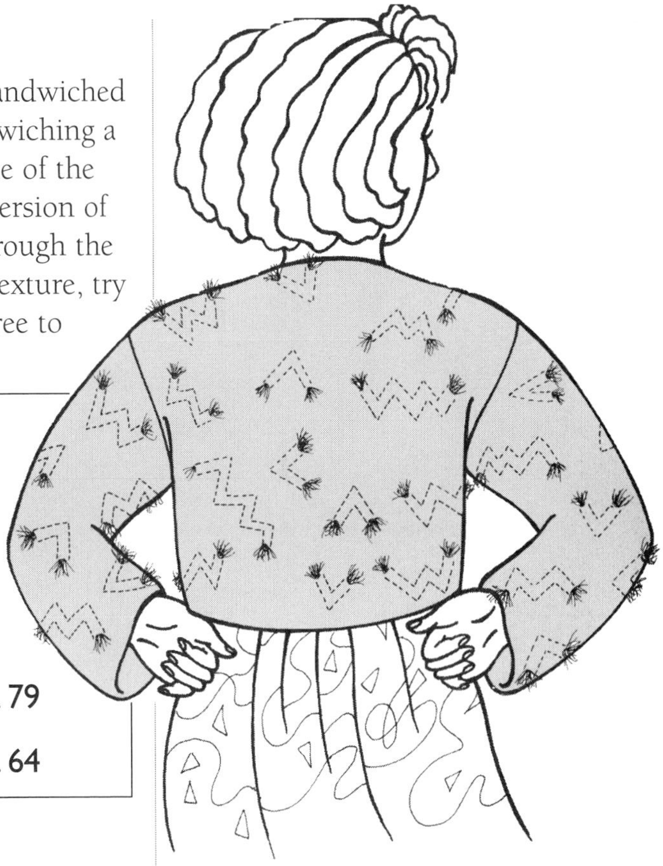

TEXTURING TECHNIQUES

(SEW) **The Trace-Over Transfer-Design Method** . p. 78

🧵 **Easy-Angle Channels**

🧵 **Twin-Needle Texturizing (optional)** . . . . p. 79

🧵 **Making Wide Serger Braid** . . . p. 64

You'll Need:

Fabric
- Pre-shrunk starched ready-made woven garment or knit sweatshirt to decorate

Needle
- 110/16 jeans

Thread
- *Top:* contrasting cordonnet of two machine embroidery threads threaded through the needle
- *Bobbin:* all-purpose sewing thread

Presser Foot
- Standard or embroidery/appliqué

Stabilizer
- 1/4 yard (0.3 m) muslin

Miscellaneous
- Seam sealant
- Beads (optional)
- Sharp embroidery scissors
- Fine crochet hook or large-eyed tapestry needle
- Beige and coordinating colors of rug yarn or wide serger braid (see Texturing Techniques Box); amount depends on how many angles you make
- Disappearing marker
- Plastic knitter's bodkin

To Texture:

1. Trace and transfer the Channel designs at the end of this chapter onto your project using the disappearing marker (see Texturing Techniques Box). Pin a piece of pinked muslin to the wrong side

Fig. 3.1: *The Easy-Angle Italian.*

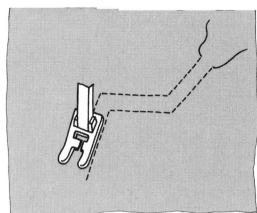

Fig. 3.2: *Straight stitch over design line, then repeat a presser-foot width away.*

A.

KNITTER'S BODKIN

SLIT RIGHT SIDE

B.

of the fabric so it extends beyond each design. If stitching this on a lapel or pocket, let the undercollar or the fabric under the pocket become the second fabric layer — no need to add muslin behind the channel.

2. Stitch over the design line using a three to three-and-a-half (six to eight stitches per inch) straight stitch. Stitch the other side of the channel guiding a presser-foot width away from the first line of stitching (Fig. 3.2). Pull threads to the back and tie them off.

SEW-HOW: *If your machine can accommodate twin needles that are 6mm apart, stitch the channels in one step (see Texturing Techniques Box).*

3. Using sharp embroidery scissors, clip both ends of the channel, cutting through the *top fabric only.* At the angle, clip the channel *underneath.* If you've stitched the channel with 6mm twin needles, clip the channel underneath without cutting the bobbin stitches.

4. Thread a knitter's bodkin with a doubled yarn or wide serger braid. Thread bodkin through the channel from the top at one end (Fig. 3.3a). At the angle, bring the yarn out through the slit underneath, then re-insert the bodkin into the other side of the channel (Fig. 3.3b). To finish, bring the yarn or cord up through the slit on the front of the channel at the other end, leaving at least a 1" (2.5cm) length at both ends of the channel. If you plan to thread beads onto the yarn, leave longer ends.

5. Using the fine crochet hook or tapestry needle, pull cordonnet ends to the back and tie them off; then dot with seam sealant. If you like, dot seam sealant on the cords, too.

Optional: Thread a bead over yarn or cord ends; then tie a knot or dot seam sealant under bead.

VARIATIONS: *Try this technique using many different colors of yarn or use cordonnet or fabric strips cut on the bias. Texture a small area of a ready-made garment or create an entire piece of fabric for a handmade project.*

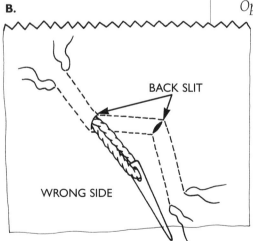

BACK SLIT

WRONG SIDE

Fig. 3.3: *Thread yarn-threaded bodkin through the channel from the top. At the angle, bring the yarn out through the slit underneath, then re-insert the bodkin into the other side of the channel.*

HELTER SKELTER SERGED SQUARES

We chose the easy route for this patchwork shirt. All the patches came from one piece of chambray printed with solid and plaid squares. Even the square sizes were determined by the fabric.

TEXTURING TECHNIQUES

- **Satin Stitch Strategy (optional)** . . . . p. 74
- **Free-Machine Embroidery** . . . . p. 67
- **Attaching a Single Bead by Machine** . . . . p. 59
- **Button Sewing — But Not by Hand** . . . . p. 62
- **"Satin Serging" a Narrow Rolled Edge** . . . . p. 76
- **"Satin Serging" Strategy** . . . . . p. 75

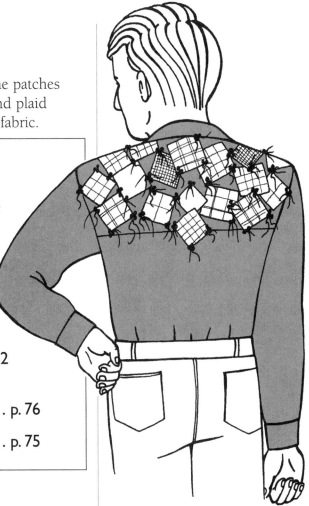

Fig. 3.4: *Helter Skelter Serged Squares.*

You'll Need:

Fabric
- Pre-shrunk starched ready-made garment to decorate
- 1/2 yard (46cm) patchwork
- Plaid fabric or scraps (we used 37 patches, each approximately 2-1/2" (6.5cm) square)

Needle
- 80/12 universal
- 90/14 universal

Thread
- *Top and bobbin:* monofilament
- *Serger needle:* color-coordinating all-purpose serger thread
- *Upper looper:* color-coordinating Woolly Nylon
- *Lower looper:* color-coordinating all-purpose serger thread

Presser Feet
- Embroidery
- Rolled hem

Miscellaneous
- Fabric shears
- Pins
- Seam sealant
- Embroidery scissors
- Glue stick
- Paper napkin
- Rotary cutter, board, and clear plastic ruler
- An assortment of colorful, different-shaped beads

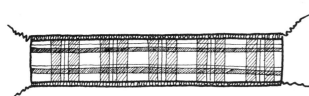

Fig. 3.5: *Serge narrow rolled edges along the two long sides of the strips.*

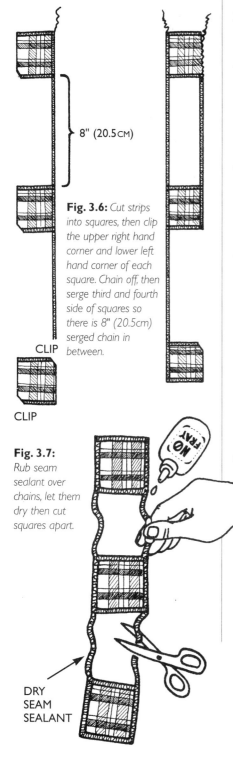

8" (20.5cm)

Fig. 3.6: *Cut strips into squares, then clip the upper right hand corner and lower left hand corner of each square. Chain off, then serge third and fourth side of squares so there is 8" (20.5cm) serged chain in between.*

CLIP

CLIP

Fig. 3.7: *Rub seam sealant over chains, let them dry then cut squares apart.*

DRY SEAM SEALANT

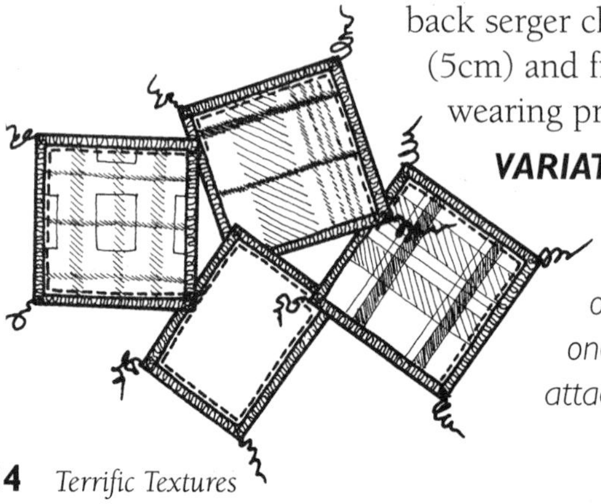

Fig. 3.8: *Freely stitch into the corners and around the inside edges of the rolled edge. Add colorful buttons and beads at each corner. Trim back serged chains to about 2" (10cm).*

To Texture:

1. Using your rotary cutter, board, and ruler, cut two 2"- (5cm) wide fabric strips across the grain. If your fabric has preprinted patches or is a plaid, cut strips the width of the pattern plus 1/4" (6mm) beyond the design.

2. Serge a narrow rolled edge on the two long sides of the strips (Fig. 3.5; see Texturing Techniques Box).

3. Cut strips into 2" (5cm) patches. If using pre-printed or plaid fabric, cut patches with a 1/4" (6mm) seam allowance on either side of the design. Clip across the upper right hand corner and lower left hand corner of each square. This way the square fits smoothly under the presser foot while the feed dogs grab the fabric.

4. Chain off at least a 4" (10cm) length, then create a narrow rolled edge on one of the raw sides of the first patch. Chain off another 8" (20.5cm) and start the next patch (Fig. 3.6). Continue in this way until you have serged the third side of each patch.

5. Turn your "kite tail" around and repeat for the last side of the patches. Pour out seam sealant on a paper napkin, dip your index finger in it, then roll the entire length of each serged chain between your thumb and index finger, lightly covering the chain in sealant. Let the sealant dry, then cut the patches apart so there are 4" (10cm) chains hanging off the four corners (Fig. 3.7).

SEW-HOW: *If you don't have a serger, you may satin-stitch the four sides of your patches as described in steps one through five. Because your sewing machine does not chain off as the serger does, cut threads off clean at the corners of each patch after the seam sealant is dry (Fig. 3.8).*

6. Arrange and pin patches on the shirt yoke so that they look as though they have fallen off the shoulders, letting parts of the shirt show through. Add other patches to cuffs, pockets, or pocket flaps. Remove pins, then glue stick patches in place.

7. Set your sewing machine for straight free-machine embroidery using monofilament thread top and bobbin and your darning foot (see Texturing Techniques Box). Freely stitch into the corners and around the inside edges of the edgestitching that's visible on each square. Next add beads and buttons at the corners, sewing them in place by hand or machine (see Texturing Techniques Box). Trim back serger chains to approximately 2" (5cm) and fight your daughter for wearing privileges.

VARIATIONS: *Rather than using patches or plaids, raid your scrap bag and use a variety of fabrics that complement one another. Collect and attach designer labels, too.*

Clockwise from upper left:
Peek-A-Button Vest, *Chapter One;*
It's-A-Miracle, *Chapter Three;*
Easy-Angle Italian Cording, *Chapter Three;*
Scrap-Saver's Removable Yoke, *Chapter Two;*
Linen Collar *(by Jan Saunders; described in Designer Showcase Key);*
Petroglyph Pets, *Chapter One.*

Clockwise from upper left:
Scrap Happy, *Chapter Two;*
When-You-Hate-to-Turn-Corners Cutwork Vest, *Chapter One;*
Curves and Corners, *Chapter Two;*
Slap-Dash and Patch, *Chapter Two;*
Zippy Doodles, *Chapter One.*

Designer Showcase

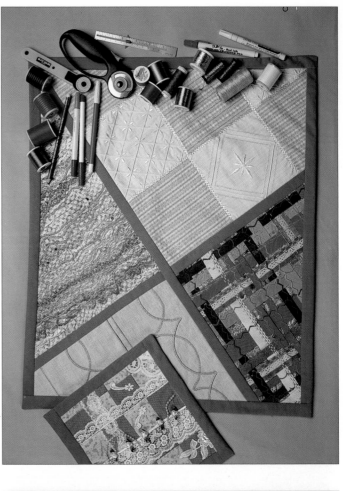

Clockwise from top:
Winging It,
Jill McCloy;
Stripe-Easy-
Stitch Wander,
Susan Rock;
Serged Rolled-
Hem Pintuck with
Soutache Braid,
April Dunn;
The Wright Stuff,
Joellen Reinhardt;
An Unfinished
Piece of Playing;
Linda McGehee.

Clockwise from
upper left corner
(outer to inner):
Hangy-Dangy
Medallions,
April Dunn;
Primary Pizazz,
*Gretchen
Heinlein-Wilson;*
Crazy-Eight Fringe,
Grace Johnson;
On the Border,
Lynn Browne;
Twix Heaven and Hell,
Angie Jachimowski;
Quilted Serger Plaid,
April Dunn;
Miracles From
Memory Craft 8000,
Mary Corollo;
Decorating the
Edges and Between,
Amy Doggett;
Just Doodling Around,
Diana Cedolia;
Potpourri,
Dori Nanry;
Hodge-Podge
Excitement,
Marilyn Gatz.

Clockwise from upper left:
Hot Stuff Lace, *Deborah Casteel;*
Woven Wonder, *Cathie Moore;*
Glamour Vest, *Patsy Shields;*
Fun with Fiber-Etch, *Michele Hester;*
Wild Bill Rides Again!, *Nancy Bednar.*

Left and right:
Hearts and Flowers, *Lynette Whicker.*
Top: Go With the Flow, *Joyce Drexler.*
Middle: Fastube Texture, *Sandra Benfield.*
Bottom: A Trunk Show, *Jan Nunn.*

Clockwise from upper left:
Quilted Cowgirl, *Jackie Dodson;*
Fringin' and Bobbin Along, *Jackie Dodson;*
Guatemalan Cowpoke Vest, *Jan Saunders;*
Classy Cowboy Vest, *Jackie Dodson;*
Mola in Reverse, *Jan Saunders.*

Clockwise from upper left: Warp-and Woof-Wear, *Chapter Two;* Flowering Denim, *Chapter Three;* Helter Skelter Serged Squares, *Chapter Three;* Breaking the Boundaries, *Chapter Two.*

IT'S-A-MIRACLE

The New Home Sewing Machine Company offers an accessory called the Miracle Stitcher. Although it is made only for this machine, we have adapted this texturing idea to any zigzag machine. The following are generic instructions. If you have the Miracle Stitcher, read the instructions that come with the accessory, then practice and use our design if you wish.

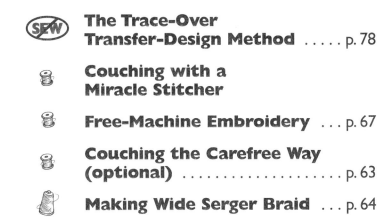

TEXTURING TECHNIQUE

- **The Trace-Over Transfer-Design Method** ..... p. 78
- **Couching with a Miracle Stitcher**
- **Free-Machine Embroidery** ... p. 67
- **Couching the Carefree Way (optional)** .... p. 63
- **Making Wide Serger Braid** ... p. 64

You'll Need:

Fabric
- Pre-shrunk starched ready-made garment to decorate

Needle
- 90/14 jeans or stretch

Thread
- *Top:* monofilament or all-purpose sewing thread to match yarn
- *Bobbin:* all-purpose sewing thread to match project

Presser Foot
- Darning or Miracle Stitcher

Stabilizer
- Tear-away

Miscellaneous
- Seam sealant
- Disappearing chalk
- Embroidery scissors
- Slubby cotton or washable yarn, or wide serger braid (see Texturing Techniques Box)
- Large-eyed tapestry needle or fine crochet hook

Fig. 3.9:
It's-A-Miracle.

To Texture:

1. Transfer the It's-A-Miracle design at the end of this chapter using the traditional trace-over method (see Texturing Techniques Box), or do what Jackie did when she couldn't find her dressmaker's carbon and empty ballpoint pen. Trace the design onto tear-away stabilizer and pin it to the wrong side of the fabric. Set your machine for free-machine embroidery and stitch over the design

through the tear-away. The stitching transfers the design so you can see it on the right side of the fabric; the yarn embroidery will later cover it up. Before adding this texture to your finished project, test and perfect your technique on fabric similar in weight.

2. If you have the Miracle Stitcher, set it up and freely couch over the yarn as explained in your instructions. If you don't, set your machine up for free-machine embroidery by dropping or covering the feed dogs and putting on the darning foot (see Texturing Techniques Box). Use a stitch width that covers the yarn, or if you prefer, use a straight stitch. Practice first.

3. Starting at the top of the design, lay the yarn in your lap and pull the free end up and under the darning foot so the yarn is under the needle. Hold the yarn end with your left hand. Anchor the yarn or braid with several stitches, clipping the yarn end off at the fabric. Now freely move your work, following the design lines while guiding the yarn with your right hand and couching the yarn down over the design line as you go. When changing direction, stop with the needle down, pivot your work, then continue.

4. To finish, clip threads and carefully remove the stabilizer. Dot thread ends with seam sealant. In some areas, you may want to pull yarn to the back using a large-eyed tapestry needle or fine crochet hook.

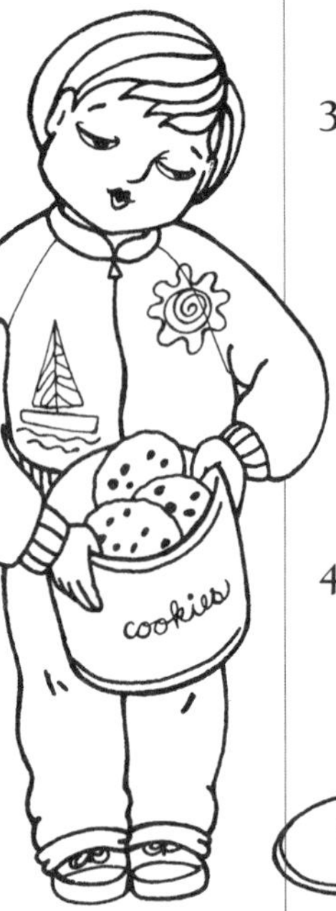

Fig. 3.10: *Couched fusible serger braid (made using fusible thread in the lower looper) creates an effect similar to the Miracle Stitcher. Designs from coloring books make good choices for children's clothes.*

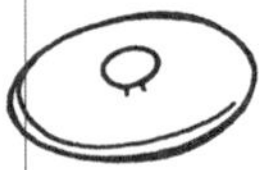

VARIATIONS: *Create a similar look by making soft serger braid using fusible thread in the lower looper (see Texturing Techniques Box), arranging braid, then fusing it down on the fabric. Couch over braid freely by machine, or use your embroidery/appliqué or braiding foot (see Texturing Techniques Box). Look for designs in coloring books, your children's or grandchildren's art work, and crewel embroidery designs (Fig. 3.10).*

Fig. 3.11: *Flowering Denim.*

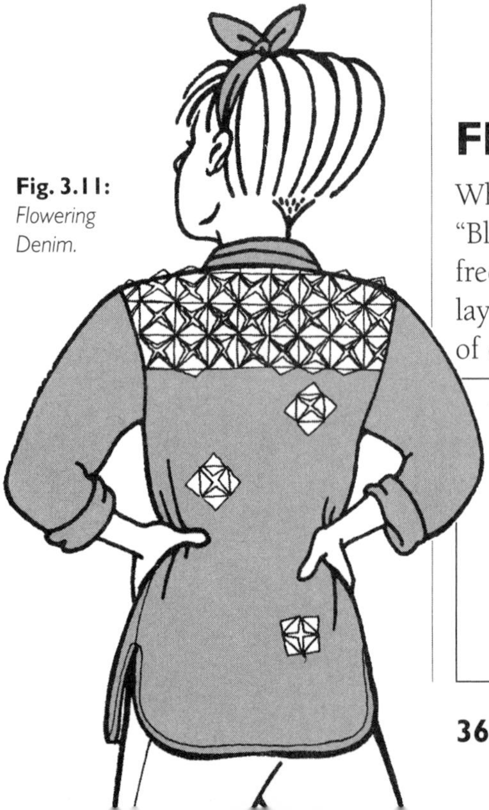

FLOWERING DENIM

When we look at this piece, we think of blooming fabric (see "Blooming Fabric" in Chapter Five), an embellishment technique frequently taught in sewing classes. But instead of clipping the outer layers to reveal several more layers beneath, we added fabric squares of denim on the surface.

TEXTURING TECHNIQUES

Flowering Denim Squares

Couching the Carefree Way . . . p. 63

Making Narrow Serger Cord . . . . p. 65

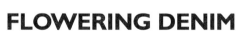

You'll Need:

Fabric
- Pre-shrunk starched ready-made woven garment or knit sweatshirt to decorate
- Denim or sweatshirt scraps in assorted colors and degrees of fading (we found that old jeans and sweatshirts work well)

Needle
- 90/14 jeans

Thread
- *Top and bobbin:* color-coordinating all-purpose sewing thread; monofilament; red all-purpose sewing thread

Presser Feet
- Embroidery/appliqué
- Cording or narrow braiding

Miscellaneous
- Seam sealant
- Red #5 pearl cotton
- Narrow serger cord (see Texturing Techniques Box)
- Disappearing marker or chalk
- Rotary cutter, board, and clear ruler

To Texture:

1. Cut denim scraps on the bias and into 2" (10cm) squares. If using sweatshirting, cut squares across the grain. Each finished "flower" ends up 1-1/2" (4cm) square, so measure the yoke and other areas to which you will be adding squares to determine how many you will need (we used 84 squares for our shirt). Then cut out at least another dozen to add where necessary.

2. Mark the sewing lines on the right side of half of the squares, as shown in Figure 3.12. Stack a marked square on top of an unmarked square, wrong sides together, and sew along the first sewing line (Fig. 3.12). Continue stacking and sewing pairs of squares this way, feeding them one after another under the presser foot and leaving threads connected between each square.

3. Cut threads to separate squares, unfold each pair, and then stitch the pairs into strips sewing on the second line, making each strip long enough to cover the yoke (Fig. 3.13). Once in strips, sew strips together along the third stitching line to create the "flowering" yardage.

4. Find the center of the area to be decorated and the center of the yardage and pin them together. Smooth the yardage from the center down over your project. At the back of the neckline, we left the squares that extended over the collar stand. We also extended the front sections of the yardage down past the edge of the yoke. Using monofilament thread top and bobbin, baste around the perimeter of the "flowering" piece to attach it to the project.

5. Rethread your machine with red all-purpose sewing thread. If you have a narrow braiding or cording foot, or a hole in your

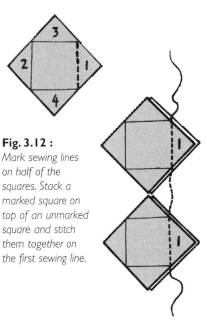

Fig. 3.12 :
Mark sewing lines on half of the squares. Stack a marked square on top of an unmarked square and stitch them together on the first sewing line.

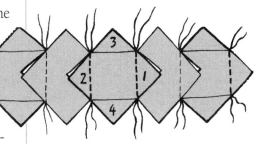

Fig. 3.13:
Sew strips together on the second sewing line.

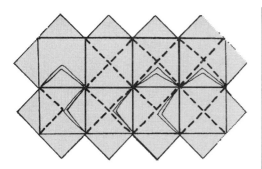

Fig. 3.14: *Couch over pearl cotton or narrow serged cord, creating a grid and attaching flower squares simultaneously.*

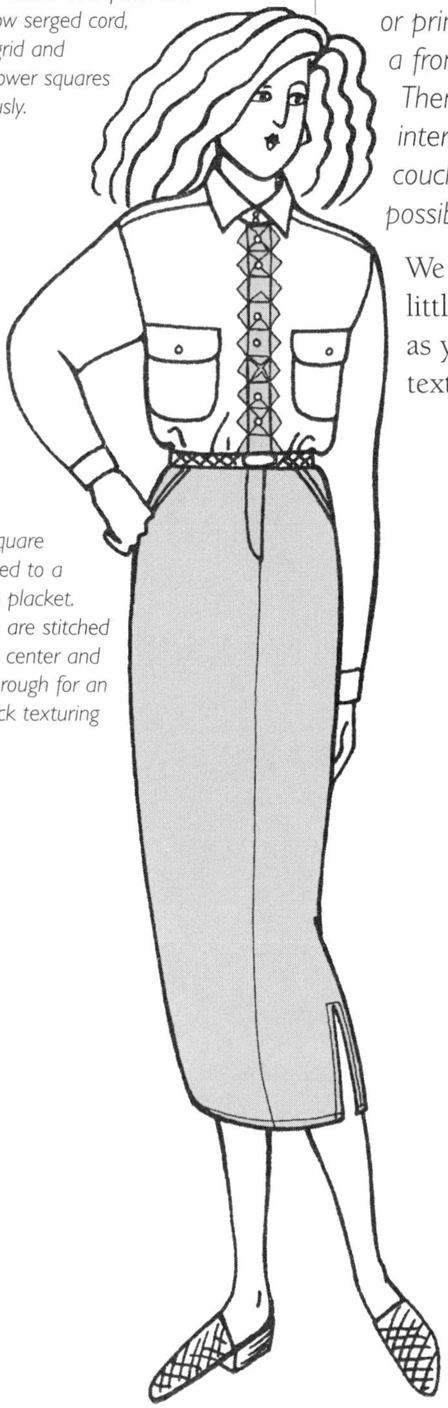

Fig. 3.15:
Flowering square strip attached to a front blouse placket. Buttonholes are stitched through the center and buttoned through for an exciting quick texturing idea.

embroidery foot, thread pearl cotton or narrow serged cord (see Texturing Techniques Box) through the foot or guide in the foot. Now couch over cord diagonally through the squares to make an "X" across the center of each square using a two-length (13 stitches per inch) and two-width zigzag to produce a diagonal grid on the yoke. This also attaches the "flowering" yardage to the project (Fig. 3.14). Pull threads and cords to the underside, tie them off, then dot with seam sealant.

VARIATIONS: *Rather than using denim, use brightly colored silk or printed cotton squares. Use one row of "flowering" squares down a front placket, stitching buttonholes through square centers. Then repeat on other design lines of the garment to create visual interest. Rather than couching a grid across each square, simply couch around each individual square — so many fast, colorful possibilities (Fig. 3.15).*

We hope we've given you some creative inspiration and had a little fun with our raised textures. Use Chapters Four and Five as your quick reference to the basics of texturing and the many texturing possibilities — everything from A to Z!

Chapter 3 Patterns

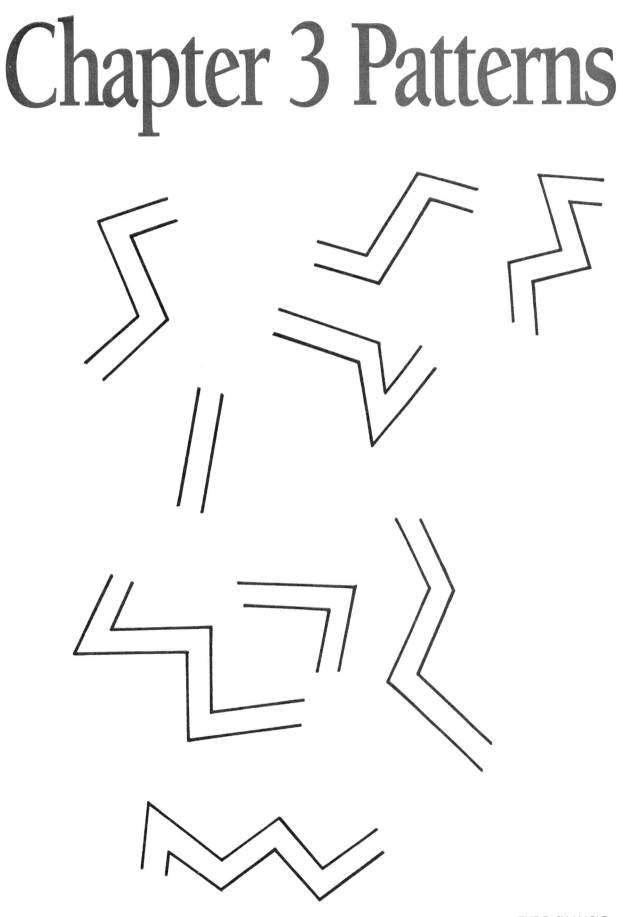

THE EASY-ANGLE
ITALIAN CHANNEL DESIGNS.

CENTER OF DESIGN

IT'S-A-MIRACLE DESIGN (THIS IS
ONLY HALF THE PATTERN SO DRAW
THE OTHER HALF AS MIRROR IMAGE
TO THE FIRST).

Doodle Page

POSSIBLE TEXTURING PROJECTS

Garment I'd Like to Texture	Technique	Page#	Sketch of Project
1.			
2.			
3.			
4.			
5.			

TOOLS, TRAPPINGS, AND OTHER TIPS

A Terrific Textures Tutorial

To create new textures, we need tools. Start with a clean and oiled sewing machine and serger. Then add needles, presser feet (there's one for every need), notions, the right threads, and some clever stabilizers and fusibles.

Before you know it you'll be creating textures by the dozens. "Treat Your Textures Right," at the end of the chapter, will show how to keep each of your creations in tip-top shape, starting with instructions for handling the fabric or garment before you add texture. Use this chapter for reference as you work through the techniques in the rest of the book.

Chapter 4

A WORD ABOUT NEEDLES

The best needle to use on any sewing machine or serger is a new one, so change it with every project. The needle tables at the end of this chapter (Table 4.1: American and European Equivalent Needle Sizes and Table 4.2: Needle Point Types) should help you coordinate your needle selection with your fabric.

THE IMPORTANCE OF PRESSER FEET

Because texturing lends itself to the creative uses of specialty presser feet, we find the following are as helpful as they are fun to use.

Sewing Machine Presser Feet
- blindhem/edge-stitch
- embroidery/appliqué
- pintuck (Fig. 4.2)*
- standard zigzag
- braiding or cording for couching narrow cord
- darning
- fringe (Fig. 4.1)*
- pearls and piping*
- walking*

Serger (²/₃- or ³/₄-thread) Presser Feet
- standard
- shirring/gathering*
- rolled edge foot (sometimes you need a rolled edge plate, too)
- pearl/sequin or beading (Fig. 4.3)*
- piping*
- elasticator*

* not usually a standard accessory foot; check with your local dealer for availability for your make and model

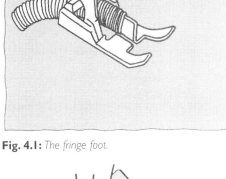

Fig. 4.1: *The fringe foot.*

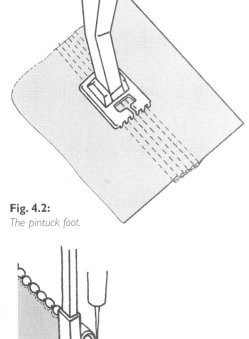

Fig. 4.2:
The pintuck foot.

SOMETIMES A GREAT NOTION (Can Make All the Difference)

Here are some lists of basic tools that should be stocked in your sewing area. Making sure you have these items on hand will help make your sewing and serging easier and more enjoyable.

Special Notions for Special Needs
- embroidery hoop for free-machine embroidery and quilting
- liquid seam sealant—use either Dritz's Fray Check, Aleene's Stop Fraying or Sullivan's Fray Stoppa to prevent raveling on the edge of laces or trim. Use it to reinforce cut edges of a buttonhole, or to prevent raw edges or serged threads from unraveling
- seam ripper for un-sewing
- surgical seam ripper for quickly ripping serged stitches
- thread nets for serger cones
- extra spool or cone holder for unusual threads and cords
- fine crochet hook or large-eyed tapestry needle for pulling threads to the back

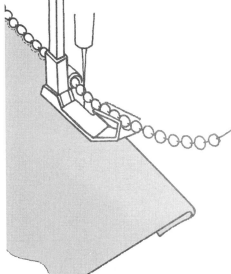

Fig. 4.3: *A serger beading or pearl/sequin foot.*

Fig. 4.4: *A knitter's bodkin is used to thread cord through drawstrings and other openings.*

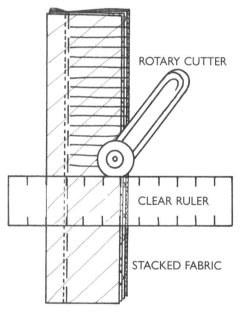

ROTARY CUTTER

CLEAR RULER

STACKED FABRIC

Fig. 4.5: *A rotary cutter and clear ruler are used to cut through stacked fabric to create fringe.*

- knitter's bodkin or ribbon threading for threading cord through channels and casings (Fig. 4.4)

Cutting Tools

- rotary cutter, board, and clear ruler or straight edge (Fig. 4.5) —we sometimes use wave and pinking blades to create more interest
- fine embroidery scissors
- appliqué (pelican) scissors

Marking Tools

- disappearing marker—line vanishes in 24-48 hours or washes out with clear cold water
- disappearing chalk—marks well on dark fabrics; line vanishes in four days or when ironed over
- black fine-point permanent Pigma pen (available at quilt and craft stores) or fine point Sharpie marker
- dressmaker's carbon and an empty ballpoint pen for transferring designs
- heat-transfer pen for transferring designs (see "Transferring Designs with Ease" in Chapter Five: Texturing A to Z)

TEXTURING THREADS, CORDS, FLOSSES, AND RIBBONS

Open your sewing basket, thread box, or wherever you keep the inedible fiber at your household to discover the texturing possibilities there. Threads can be used through your sewing machine or serger needles; cords can be wound on and used in your bobbins; ribbons, flosses, and yarns can be couched over by hand or machine and used in your serger's upper and sometimes lower loopers.

When selecting thread for your sewing machine or serger, read the label, unwrap a little, then take a close look at it. With the exception of Woolly Nylon that has a crimped texture, it should have a smooth, even appearance. For your sewing machine, all-purpose sewing thread is generally three-ply. Serger thread, which is usually two-ply, is available on cones or tubes of 1,000 to 6,000 yards. Even though several strands of serger thread are used in a serged seam, the thread will keep the fabric and seam supple because it is generally a lighter weight than conventional all-purpose sewing thread.

Here is a list of the most common threads. As with any project, match the fiber of the fabric to the thread, cord, yarn, or floss for easy care and maintenance.

"SEW & SERGE" HOW: *One of our favorite texturing effects can be achieved by "blending" threads—threading from two to four threads through the eye of the same needle. A handy new tool used both on your sewing machine and serger is the Thread Palette. This* *four-pegged disk sits over the upper looper spool pin so two to four decorative threads can be smoothly blended. To use it on the sewing machine, use it on a cone stand. Buy the Thread Palette through your favorite sewing machine retailer or mail-order source.*

Sewing and Serging Threads

One hundred percent cotton sewing thread works well for most garment construction, provided it is colorfast and mercerized. Mercerizing increases strength, luster, and dye affinity, so it can be used for embroidery, topstitching, and buttonholes. You shouldn't experience uneven tension problems because cotton fibers are long and smooth. Cotton thread is not as strong as cotton-wrapped polyester, or 100% polyester; however, if used with the correct stitch for the fabric, cotton thread is strong enough for most fabrics and is available in weights for both the sewing machine and serger.

All-purpose cotton-wrapped polyester thread, often referred to in this book as all-purpose sewing thread, is also colorfast and mercerized, and is recommended for garment construction. This thread has slightly less sheen, is stronger, and stretches more than 100% cotton thread because of its polyester core. It is available in weights for both the sewing machine and serger.

All-purpose one hundred percent polyester thread was originally developed in the sixties and seventies so we could successfully sew knit fabrics with a straight stitch. The major brands are made with long-staple fibers (at least 2" [5cm]) and are soft and smooth but lack the sheen and luster of cotton or rayon threads. Even though polyester thread is not considered decorative thread, it works well in decorative cutwork when using Fiber-Etch Fabric Remover, a product that dissolves plant fibers, including cotton, some rayon, linen, and paper (see When-You-Hate-to-Turn-Corners Cutwork Vest in Chapter One). Polyester thread is available in weights for both the sewing machine and serger. Always test on a scrap first.

Cotton embroidery thread, which is finer than cotton sewing thread, is great for free-machine embroidery because the stitches have a nice sheen and lie smoothly on the fabric without the bulk of cotton sewing thread. Because of the cost, the limited number of yards on a spool, and its relative weakness compared to other threads, cotton embroidery thread is not generally recommended for serging.

Acrylic embroidery thread is relatively new on the home sewing market and was specifically developed for machine embroidery. It is a 50-weight static-free embroidery thread that has more shine than 100% cotton thread but less than rayon embroidery thread. This thread can be used on the serger, is available though local sewing machine dealers, and can also be used with Fiber-Etch (see the When-You-Hate-to-Turn-Corners Cutwork Vest in Chapter One).

Rayon embroidery thread is not as strong a fiber as cotton or polyester, but it is smooth. Much shinier than the previously mentioned threads, it is beautiful for decorative stitching. To prevent it from shredding and breaking, use a size 80/12 embroidery needle on light to mid-weight fabrics. On heavier fabrics, use a size 90/14 stretch, jeans, metafil, or embroidery needle. The larger needle pokes a larger hole in the fabric, while the groove in the front of the needle protects the thread from wearing against the fabric with each stitch. Rayon threads are also available in heavier six-ply weight for sensational results when topstitching, couching, and doing sashiko.

Metallic threads can be twisted, flat, wrapped around or wrapped with other fibers. A general rule for using metallic threads for free-machine embroidery or edge finishes (such as rolled edges and lettuce hems), is to use a size 80/12 embroidery or a 90/14 jeans needle to prevent splitting, separating, and breakage (see Needle Tables 4.1 and 4.2). Either one has a large enough eye to allow the thread to smoothly pass through it. The 90/14 jeans needle has a very sharp point for good fabric penetration and the groove in the front of the needle protects the thread from wearing against the fabric with each stitch. Use metallics on both your sewing machine and serger. There is a flood of metallic threads in a variety of weights, and more being introduced to the market all the time. So buy them, test them, and let us know what you've discovered.

Darning or basting thread is very fine and is often used on the bobbin for free-machine embroidery. It can be 100% cotton or 100% polyester. A lot can be wound on a bobbin, so you don't have to change bobbins with every color top thread. Because it comes in white and sometimes black, loosen the top tension so the decorative stitches lock under the fabric.

Nylon thread can be used on both the sewing machine and serger. It is extremely strong. Because of its strength and elasticity, nylon thread is mostly used in swim suit and lingerie construction.

Woolly Nylon is a texturized nylon thread that can be used on the sewing machine and serger, but is most commonly used on the serger for rolled edges. Its textured crimp fluffs out to fill in spaces between stitches on a rolled edge.

Monofilament thread is like very fine fishline and blends with other thread or fiber color, which is helpful because you don't have to rethread your machine or serger when using different color fabrics on the same project. The best we've found is 100% polyester and .004 mm in diameter—very fine for soft pliable results. Use monofilament on your sewing machine for couching and bobbin work; use it in your serger for invisible hemming; or for flatlocking to couch over ribbon, sequins, and pearls.

Topstitching and cordonnet threads are heavier than sewing threads, are available in several fiber contents, and show up well when topstitching. Use a size 90/14 stretch or larger, jeans, or topstitching needle for best results. Either thread can be used on your sewing machine for Sashiko (see "Sashiko Secrets" in Chapter Five: Texturing A to Z), or in both loopers of your serger.

Certain of today's **hand quilting threads** can be used on your sewing machine or serger because the thread fibers are generally impregnated with a glacé finish, which prevents knotting, shredding, and tangling when used by hand. Check your favorite mail-order source or write to the thread company listed in the Sources of Supplies in the back of this book to determine if it is all right to use on your machine. Older hand quilting thread used to have a wax finish that would gum-up the tension disks, so watch thread you are not sure of to make certain the wax is not separating from the thread while sewing. It comes in all-cotton or cotton-wrapped polyester with all the properties of each fiber mentioned above.

Decorative Cords, Flosses, and Ribbons

We'll try almost any fiber in our sewing machines or sergers. On a trip to visit her brother in Alaska, Jan bought a beautiful multi-ply flat rayon floss she found in a bait store which she then couched over for a sensational topstitch. Use your sewing machine to add a three-dimensional look to a surface by putting the decorative cord in the bobbin, loosening or bypassing the tension, and sewing upside down. For a dramatic edge, thread the loopers in your serger with a decorative cord and loosen the looper tensions to perfect the stitch. Because the eyelets in serger loopers are larger than the largest needle's eye, they can accommodate a variety of decorative yarns, ribbons, flosses, and ribbon flosses, too.

> **SERGING SAVVY:** Many of the decorative flosses, cords, ribbons, and yarns are on a ball or in a skein. Rewind them onto a yarn cone available through your local knitting machine dealer. If you don't have a knitting machine dealer in your neighborhood, get horizontal spool pins to attach to your serger spool pins through your favorite sewing machine dealer or mail-order source (Fig. 4.6).

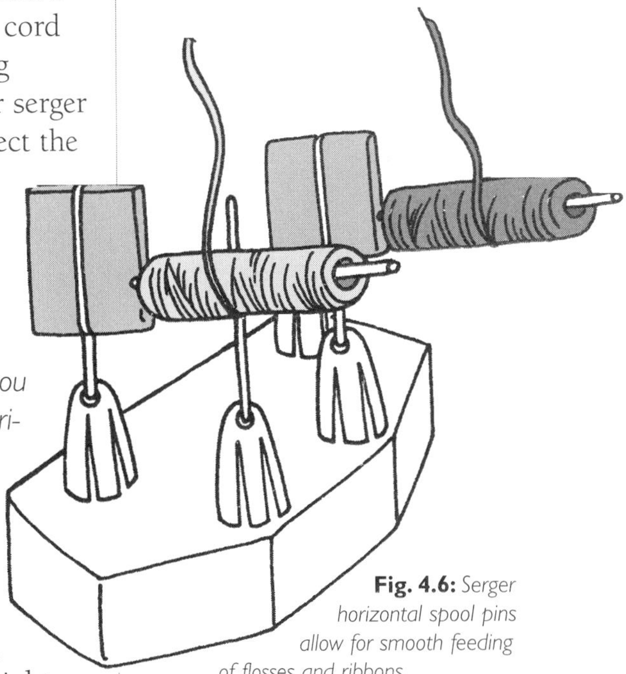

Fig. 4.6: Serger horizontal spool pins allow for smooth feeding of flosses and ribbons.

Common Cords, Flosses, and Ribbons
- pearl cotton—a twisted 100% cotton cord available on a cone, ball, or skein; the most common size is five, but it's also available in a larger size three and a finer size eight
- crochet thread—more tightly twisted than pearl cotton, this cord is available in cotton or acrylic, including variegated and metallic
- silk ribbon—an expensive soft, pliable ribbon that works beautifully in the bobbin and through the loopers; if you plan to use a lot on a project, the acrylic ribbon (often called synthetic silk) is a good alternative
- acrylic ribbon—soft and pliable like silk ribbon, but cheaper; you can hardly see the difference between the two
- rayon ribbon and ribbon floss—very shiny and soft; it drapes well and will work in the bobbin and through the loopers
- two-ply knitting machine or baby yarn—soft, smooth, and drapable, and will work best through your serger loopers; when selecting yarn, choose one with a smooth, unslubby texture, and with a tight twist

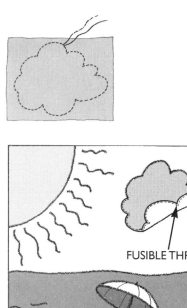

Fig. 4.7: *Use fusible thread to outline an appliqué; then cut it out and fuse-baste it onto the base fabric. Use fusible thread in your lower looper when finishing a hem edge to fuse-baste a hem.*

- fusible thread—a smooth white thread with fusing agent in it that melts and adheres to the fabric when it is pressed over; while it is not a permanent fuse, it's great for fuse-basting; use it on the bobbin to outline and fuse-baste appliqué, or in the lower looper to make a fusible serged cord (Fig. 4.7)

Of course, there are hundreds of decorative fibers, cords, ribbons, and threads available that we don't have room to list here. In addition, new ones are being introduced all the time. Treat yourself by taking a field trip to your local sewing machine dealers, fabric, and craft stores to discover what else you can use in your sewing machine and serger.

STABILIZERS

Fabrics that will be appliquéd, embroidered, monogrammed, or couched over often need a stabilizer to prevent stitches from skipping, puckering, or tunneling (when a zigzag draws the fabric into a roll that curls under the stitch). You can spray, paint, press, or pin stabilizers on. To remove, tear away, iron away, or wash away.

We used mostly woven fabrics for the texturing techniques in this book because they don't move or stretch like knit fabrics do. This does not mean you can't use knits, but if you do, remember to stabilize them for the best results. If you will be adding your texturing pieces to a knit sweatshirt, for example, use tear-away or iron-on tear-away stabilizer under the shirt to prevent stretching and stitch distortion.

Tear-away stabilizers are placed under the base fabric. Decorative stitching is done on the right side of the fabric, then the stabilizer is torn away after stitching. Easily available brands are Pellon's Stitch-n-Tear, HTC's perforated Easy-Stitch, and Sulky's Tear-Easy. For a tear-away stabilizer that removes cleanly without leaving a paper residue around the stitches, use Clotilde's No Whiskers. Sulky's Totally Stable is an iron-on tear-away stabilizer that lightly sticks to the fabric, then is easily torn off after stitching. Other tear-away options that work in an emergency (especially if you don't need to remove the stabilizer from under the stitching) are doctor's examination paper, coffee filter paper, adding machine tape, and delicatessen paper.

Iron-away stabilizers are made of a muslin-like fabric that is chemically treated to dissolve when heated by an iron, press, or hair dryer. Remember to use this stabilizer *exactly* as you are instructed on the package — improper use may damage your base fabric. Look for Michelle Pullen's Vanish-A-Way, Sulky's Heat-Away, Hot Stuff!! from Aardvark, or Vanishing Muslin from Magic Needle. Find these stabilizers at your local sewing machine dealer, fabric, craft, or mail-order sources.

Wash-away stabilizers are made of either a semi-transparent film or a strong lightweight fabric that dissolves in water. Sulky's Solvy, Speed Stitch's Wash-Away and Clotilde's Solv-it are transparent enough so you can trace over a design right onto the film.

Once placed onto the right side of the fabric, they will wash or spritz away after stitching. Madeira's Melt-A-Way and HTC's RinsAway are strong lightweight fabrics that dissolve in water.

Spray or paint-on stabilizers add a little or a lot of firmness to the fabric, depending on your needs. For light support, use spray starch or Helmar's Lite Fabric Stiffener, available in liquid and aerosol. For firmer support, paint or squeeze on Palmer/Pletsch's Perfect Sew or Tacony's Sew Stable. Sulky also gives you instructions for dissolving Solvy in water to make a paint-on stabilizer. When these products are dry, they stiffen the fabric to prevent puckering. You can remove them easily by laundering or rinsing them in water.

Cotton broadcloth works beautifully under sweater knit or other loosely knitted fabrics for hand or machine embroidery.

PAPER-BACKED FUSIBLE WEB AND OTHER FUSIBLES

Because we textured pieces of fabric that we then cut up and applied to ready-to-wear, the fusibles we used most often in this book are paper-backed fusible transfer webs. Available by the yard or cut and rolled into 1/4"-3/4" (6mm-2cm) widths, these webs fuse hems and edges, or secure larger appliqués. Look for Aleene's Hot Stitch Fusible Web, Dritz Hem-N-Trim, HTC's Trans-Web, J & R's Magic Fuse (now distributed by Dritz), Pellon's Wonder-Under, Speed Stitch's Fusible Film, or Thermo Web's HeatnBond and HeatnBond Lite. To use, just iron it on the wrong side of the fabric with the paper side up, following the manufacturer's instructions. Cut out the appliqué, peel off the paper, then fuse. Fusible web makes any fabric fusible so it's great for patching and applique.

PRESSING MATTERS: A Teflon pressing sheet is a small, translucent, non-stick pressing sheet used to prevent fusible adhesive from sticking to the iron and/or the ironing surface. Use it or release paper with fusible web, paper-backed fusible web, liquid fusible web, or as a press cloth on fabrics and threads that need lower iron temperatures, such as nylon, rayon, and acrylic.

GLUES

You know those little yellow slips of paper that stick temporarily to just about anything? Using the same kind of *pressure-sensitive adhesive,* you can transform laces, crests, appliqués, trims, ribbons, removable collars and cuffs, and even shoulder pads into removable accents for temporary enhancement or embellishment. There are a number on the market: Aleene's Tack-It Over & Over, Clotilde's Sticky Stuff, Faultless' Bead Easy Re-Apply Adhesive, Plaid's Stickit Again & Again. As with any glue, test on a seam allowance or like fabric scrap for color fastness. Here are the basic how-to's.

1. Using a disposable brush, apply glue to the wrong side of the appliqué, crest, patch, or trim.

2. Let the glue dry as recommended by the manufacturer (usually 24 hours). It will dry clear and tacky.

3. Position the item and apply hand pressure. The decoration will stick solidly to the fabric.

4. When it's time to remove the decoration, simply peel it off store it on waxed paper, then use it again. The glue stays tacky for many wearings. *Note:* Some of these glues are temporary until they have been on the garment for over 24 hours; then they become permanent. Read the label carefully.

Fabric glue stick is available through your local fabric store or through mail-order sources. We use it to temporarily glue-baste appliqués, buttons, beads, or baubles in place. We also dot glue along a cord so we can arrange and rearrange it before couching it down (see "Couching the Carefree Way" in Chapter Five: Texturing A to Z).

Permanent washable glue holds knotted ends, and other bits and pieces in your textured creations. Look for washable (but not always dry cleanable) clear solvent-based glues called Fabri Tak, EZ Fabric Glue, or Fabric Mender. White waterproof glues to look for are OK-to-Wash-It, Glu-N-Wash, or Unique Stitch.

Look for *The Crafter's Guide to Glues* by Tammy Young (Chilton, 1995) for more information.

FABRIC LAMINATING FILM

Fuse this product to a piece of fabric following the manufacturer's instructions to make the fabric waterproof—great for patio furniture, tote bags, place mats, tablecloths, shower curtains, children's gift items, slipcovers, and pillows. Some brands can be fused to each other and can be written or painted on as well. Look for HeatnBond Iron-On Flexible Vinyl and Kittrich Iron-On Clear Cover.

TREAT YOUR TEXTURES RIGHT

Pre-Shrinking Pointers

We have designed the texturing techniques in this book to be added to finished garments, so the fabrics and trims used to texture the piece must be compatible with the base garment (meaning that everything should have similar fiber contents and care instructions). We recommend pre-shrinking the base garment before you start the project. Simply follow the manufacturer's care instructions. Also pre-shrink appliqué and foundation fabrics, trims, and ribbons by soaking them in hot water and drying in the dryer.

SEW-HOW: For trims, either fold the trims and rubber band them together or fold them right on the card they're wrapped around. Then put them in a bowl of water and microwave the whole thing on high for two minutes. Once trims have cooled, rinse them in cool water and dry them in the dryer.

Caring for Your Creations

To wash your textured treasure, turn the garment inside out and either hand-wash or wash it on the gentle cycle in the automatic washer. Pop the piece in the dryer on the permanent press cycle and dry it until it's almost dry ("cooking" it on the cotton cycle isn't recommended because it will shorten the life of your project). Remove it from the dryer and finish by line drying. Press your project before wearing it to give it that fresh, "just-made" look. If you have textured a piece of fabric and made it removable by attaching snaps to the collar, cuff, or front yoke, the embellished piece can be snapped off and laundered separately from the base garment to prolong its life and beauty.

Now that you have learned about the tools and trappings involved in texturizing, look for specific how-to instructions for more than twenty-five terrific techniques in Chapter Five: Texturizing A to Z.

Table 4.1–American and European Equivalent Needle Sizes

American	European	Suggested Fabrics
8	60	Silk chiffon, organza, sheers, fine cottons, and microfibers
9	65	Tissue faille, voile, georgette, blouse-weight silks, and microfibers
10	70	Blouse and lightweight dress fabric
11	75	Knit interlock, Lyrca activewear, knit sheers, Ultrasuede and other synthetic suedes and leathers, midweight microfibers
12	80	Suitweight silks, linens, and wools
14	90	Denim, topstitching with topstitching thread, heavy duck cloth, midweight real leather and suede
16	100	Very heavy duck cloth, some upholstery fabrics, upholstery vinyl
18	110	Some decorative hemstitching; use if the size 16/100 breaks
–	120	Decorative hemstitching; use if the size 18/110 breaks

Reprinted from *Jan Saunders' Wardrobe Quick-Fixes*, Chilton, 1995, p. 144.

Table 4.2–Needle Point Types

Classification	Type
General Purpose Sewing Machine Needles	
15 × 1H 130/705H	**Universal:** Cross between a sharp point and a ballpoint tip used on most knits and wovens. This needle is most widely available and sews beautifully on the majority of fabrics. Twin-needle sizes available in 1.6 12/80, 2.0 12/80, 2.5 12/80, 3.0 12/80, 3.0 14/90, 4.0 12/80, 4.0 14/90, 6.0 16/100; triple needles available in 2.5 12/80 and 3.0 12/80.
15 × 1SP 130/705 SUK	**Ballpoint:** A round-tipped needle designed for use on heavy knits such as power net. The ball point slips easily between the loops in the knit fabric without skipping stitches or snagging. Not as widely available as the universal but available in sizes 10/70–16/100.
Blue Tip 130/705HS 130/705HPS (Pfaff) Sears "Q" Singer 2045	**Stretch:** Has a sharper point than a universal needle, with a deeper scarf; which aids in stitch formation to prevent skipped stitches. Recommended for swimwear knits, Lycra, synthetic suede, free-machine embroidery, and some microfibers. Often has a blue tip or shaft for easy identification. Twin-needle sizes available in 2.5 11/75 and 4.0 12/80.

Classification	Type

General Purpose Sewing Machine Needles (continued)

15 × 1DE
130/705HJ

Denim or Jeans: Sharp point to penetrate closely woven fabrics easily, without breaking. Recommended for denim, corduroy, and upholstery fabric. Single needles available in sizes 10/70-18/110. Twin needle sizes available in 4.0 16/100.

15 × 1 or 705B
(B for Bernina)
130/705 HM
Singer 2020
Microtex

Sharp or Pierce Point: A sharp needle used for sewing woven silks and microfibers. The small sizes (from 8/60-14/90) produce a very straight line of stitching. Also recommended for French hand sewing by machine on fine cottons and linen. Often has a violet shaft for easy identification. Bernina owners, read inside the hook cover to see if this needle is recommended for your machine.

Specialty Sewing Machine Needles

130/705 HM
Metafil

Embroidery: Designed for use with metallic, novelty, and machine embroidery threads; available in sizes 11/75 and 14/90. This needle has larger eye and groove dimensions to prevent threads from splitting and shredding. It also has a deeper scarf for better stitch formation and to prevent skipped stitches. The sharp point avoids damage to the fabric and other threads when embroidering. Often has a red shaft or band for easy identification. Twin-needle sizes available in 2.0 11/75 and 3.0 11/75.

705 Handicap

Handicap: *Sharp* point with a self-threading eye available in sizes 12/80 and 14/90.

130/705 HQ

Quilting: Durable tapered point for sewing the many seams required for piecing without damaging the fabric. Currently available in sizes 75 and 90. Often has a green shaft or band for easy identification.

130/705H
130/705HS
SPRING

Spring: Available in universal sizes 10/70-14/90, stretch 11/75 or 14/90, and denim 16/100, they have darning springs around them. Used for free-machine embroidery, darning, and quilting for better visibility. When using this needle, you don't need a darning foot.

15 × 1ST
130/705N

Topstitch: The eye and front groove of the needle are twice the size of a normal 11/75 or 14/90 needle to accommodate heavy topstitching thread. Some topstitching needles have sharp tips to produce the straightest topstitch.

15 × 1LL
130/705HLL
130/705NTW

Wedge Point or Leather: Available in sizes 10/70-18/110, this large-eye needle has a wedge point to penetrate leather. The point slices into the leather rather than perforating it.

130/705 H WING

Wing: The needle has wings running the length of the shaft to poke a large hole when hemstitching. The stitch goes in and out of the same hole, binding it open after stitching. Twin wing is available in size 16/100.

Reprinted from *Jan Saunders' Wardrobe Quick-Fixes*, Chilton, 1995, pp. 144-145.

Chapter 5

TEXTURING
A TO Z

More Than Twenty-Five Techniques To Try

For easy reference, the instructions for texturing techniques used throughout the book are in this section. If a technique is used only once, it appears in the instructions for the texturing piece (e.g., see the When-You-Hate-To-Turn-Corners Cutwork Vest in Chapter One). Remember, before stitching anything on your finished piece, we recommend testing the technique first on a scrap using the same fabric, thread, stitch, tension settings, and stabilizer as you would on the finished piece.

APPLIQUÉ FOUR EASY WAYS

Simply put, appliquéing is placing fabric on fabric and attaching it, but there are many ways to do this. Our book gives you a sampling of techniques, including the following four basic methods, which we use on several texturing pieces: appliqué with dramatic couched edges, appliqué with turned-back edges, cut-away appliqué, and simple fused appliqué with satin-stitched edges.

Other appliqué techniques can be found in individual projects. In Chapter Two, for example, the Scrap-Saver's Removable Yoke uses sheer-overlay appliqué, and the Petroglyph Pets in Chapter One are made with a form of reverse appliqué.

Appliqué with Dramatic Couched Edges

Use this technique for a raised edge to your appliqué.

Machine Readiness Checklist

FABRIC APPLIQUÉ	COUCHED EDGES
• *Stitch:* zigzag	same
• *Foot:* embroidery/appliqué	braiding, or sequins and ribbon
• *Stitch length:* 1-2 (13-24 stitches per inch)	same
• *Stitch width:* 1-2	wide enough to cover cord
• *Needle:* appropriate for fabric	same
• *Thread:* all-purpose sewing thread to match cord	same
• *Tension:* normal	same
• *Accessories:* none	yarn or serged cord
• *Miscellaneous:* paper-backed fusible web	

1. Make a fabric fusible by backing it with paper-backed fusible web (see "Paper-Backed Fusible Web and Other Fusibles" in Chapter Four). We usually back a larger-than-necessary piece of fabric for our appliqués because it's easier to work with and then we're assured that the entire appliqué is fused with web. Draw the mirror image of your appliqué onto the release paper, then cut it out.

2. Remove the release paper and fuse it to the base fabric following the manufacturer's instructions.

3. Attach the fabric appliqué with an open zigzag stitch around the perimeter of the appliqué guide that zigs into the appliqué on one side and zags just over the appliqué edge on the other (Fig. 5.1).

4. To couch the edges, place the yarn or serged cord in the braiding or ribbon and sequin foot and couch around the perimeter of the appliqué (Fig. 5.2). Pull loose threads to the back using a large-eyed tapestry needle, fine latch hook, or needle threader and tie them off. Clip yarn or cord off at the fabric.

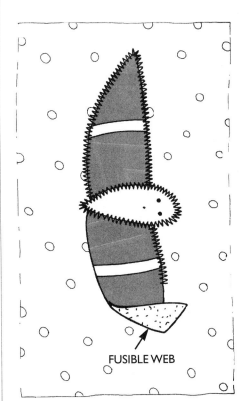

FUSIBLE WEB

Fig. 5.1: *Outline the appliqué perimeter using an open zigzag stitch.*

Fig. 5.2: *Couch yarn or serger braid around appliqué, over open zigzag stitches.*

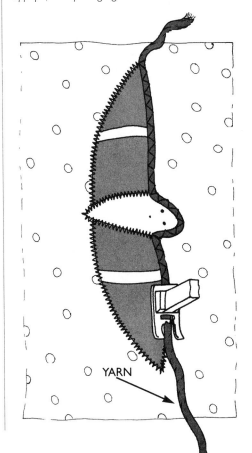

YARN

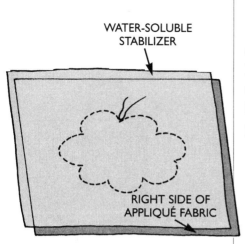

Fig. 5.3: *Stack water-soluble stabilizer on top of appliqué fabric, right sides together and stitch around the appliqué.*

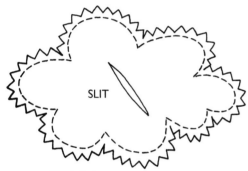

Fig. 5.4: *Cut out appliqué ⅛" (3mm) outside the stitching line. To notch the curves, trim with pinking shears. Slit water-soluble stabilizer and turn appliqué through the slit.*

Fig. 5.5: *Dot appliqué back with glue stick, stitch around appliqué with a blindhem or blanket stitch.*

WATER-SOLUBLE STABILIZER (label in Fig. 5.3)

RIGHT SIDE OF APPLIQUÉ FABRIC (label in Fig. 5.3)

SLIT (label in Fig. 5.4)

BLIND HEM STITCH (label in Fig. 5.5)

SEW-HOW: *If this appliqué will not be worn with the wrong side against the skin, use monofilament thread, top and bobbin.*

Appliqué with Turned-Back Edges

For soft results that won't pull out, Jackie stabilizes and turns back an appliquéd edge using water-soluble stabilizer. Remember, choose fabrics that can be wetted.

Machine Readiness Checklist

- *Stitch:* blindhem; blanket
- *Foot:* embroidery/appliqué or edge-stitch
- *Stitch length:* 1-1.5 (20 stitches per inch); appropriate for stitch
- *Stitch width:* 1-1.5
- *Needle:* appropriate for the fabric
- *Thread:* cotton embroidery thread to match appliqué or monofilament
- *Tension:* normal
- *Stabilizer:* water soluble
- *Miscellaneous:* Teflon pressing sheet, glue stick

1. Stack one each of the appliqué fabric and water-soluble stabilizer, right sides together. Stitch around the appliqué design (Fig. 5.3).

2. Cut out appliqué about ⅛" (3mm) outside the stitching line. If appliqué has curves, cut it out using pinking shears to automatically notch the curve (Fig. 5.4).

3. Cut a slit through the water-soluble stabilizer, turning the appliqué through the slit (see Fig. 5.4). Set your iron on the wool setting. With the stabilizer side down and against the Teflon pressing sheet, use the tip of the iron and carefully press around the perimeter of the appliqué from the top side.

4. To position on fabric surface, dot glue stick on the back of each appliqué. Stitch the appliqué onto the base fabric using a machine blind hem stitch or a blanket stitch (Fig. 5.5).

5. Remove the stabilizer by dipping the piece in water, following the manufacturers' instructions. With the stabilizer removed, the appliqué is soft and the edges are securely turned back so they will not pull away from the stitching.

Cut-Away Appliqué

For more inspiration for the cut-away appliqué technique, look in the Designer's Showcase (in the color pages) for "A Trunk Show" by designer Jan Nunn.

1. Layer three or four contrasting or complementary fabrics so the identifiable print is on the top or the bottom of the sandwich. This will be your design line.

2. Set your machine for free-machine embroidery (see "Free-Machine Embroidery and Quilting" later in this chapter), and a

one-width zigzag. You will be outlining the design from either the top or bottom fabrics. For example, Jan freely outlined all the butterfly wings and bodies on this piece (Fig. 5.6).

3. After the outlining is done, use a sharp pair of embroidery scissors and trim close to the outline stitch, first cutting through only one layer of fabric to expose the one underneath. Next, somewhere else cut through two layers of fabric to reveal a second fabric underneath. Continue cutting away, cutting through one, two, or three layers randomly and letting the fabrics, colors, and textures underneath peek out between the top shapes.

4. For more texture, couch decorative cords or threads, or satin stitch over the edges of the previous outline stitching (see "Couching the Carefree Way" later in this chapter).

Simple Fused Appliqué with Satin-Stitched Edges

Machine Readiness Checklist

- *Stitch:* zigzag
- *Foot:* embroidery/appliqué
- *Stitch length:* 0.5-0.8 (60 stitches per inch [fine setting])
- *Stitch width:* 2.5-4mm
- *Needle:* 80/12 embroidery or 90/14 jeans
- *Thread:* cotton or rayon embroidery thread in top; darning or basting thread in bobbin
- *Tension:* upper tension slightly loosened
- *Miscellaneous:* paper-backed fusible web (this usually adds enough stiffness to the appliqué to serve the purpose of stabilizer)

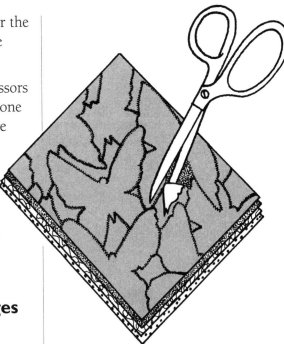

Fig. 5.6: *Freely outline the design from the top or bottom fabric layer. Trim close to the outline of each motif, first cutting through one fabric layer; trim around another motif cutting through two fabric layers, revealing fabrics underneath.*

1. Make a fabric appliqué fusible by backing it with paper-backed fusible web (see "Paper-Backed Fusible Web and Other Fusibles" in Chapter Four). We usually back a larger-than-necessary piece of fabric for our appliqués because it's easier to work with and then we're assured that the entire appliqué is fused with web. Draw the mirror image of your appliqué onto the release paper, then cut it out.

2. Remove the release paper and fuse it to the base fabric following the manufacturer's instructions.

   SEW-HOW: *When you remove the release paper from a large piece of fabric, keep the paper and re-use it for a paper press cloth so the fusible web won't gum up your iron or ironing board.*

   SERGING SAVVY: *For larger appliqués, don't use paper-backed fusible web. Instead, finish around the edges with a narrow rolled hem or a short balanced three-thread stitch using decorative thread or cord in the upper looper (see "'Satin Serging' Strategy" later in this chapter) and fusible thread in the lower looper. To attach the appliqué to a base fabric, tuck loose thread ends under the appliqué and stitch-in-the-ditch at the inside edge of the serged narrow rolled edge. To attach a*

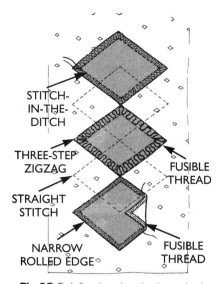

STITCH-IN-THE-DITCH

THREE-STEP ZIGZAG

FUSIBLE THREAD

STRAIGHT STITCH

NARROW ROLLED EDGE

FUSIBLE THREAD

Fig. 5.7: *Tuck free threads under the appliqué and attach wider serged satin-stitched edge with matching thread and a wide three-step zigzag stitch.*

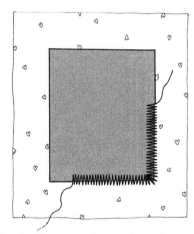

Fig. 5.8: *Place presser foot over the appliqué so the needle catches into the appliqué on the left and barely swings over the raw edge on at the right.*

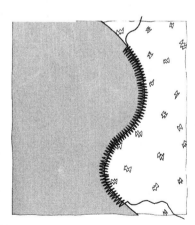

Fig. 5.9: *On a curve, stitches fan out on an outside curve.*

wider serged satin-stitched edge, use a matching thread to topstitch over the edge using a three-step zigzag or other open decorative stitch (Fig. 5.7).

3. Place the presser foot over the appliqué so the needle catches into the appliqué fabric on the left and barely swings over the raw edge on the right (Fig. 5.8). Stitches will fan on outside or inside curves (Fig. 5.9).

SEW-HOW: *To make a perfect circle, use the circle-making accessory available for your sewing machine, or tape a thumbtack to the bed of your machine the radius-distance from the needle. Place the fabric over the point of the tack, lower the foot, and place a rubber eraser or cork over the point of the tack. Sew. The tack works like the center point of a compass so the fabric feeds in a perfect circle while the satin stitches fan out automatically (Fig. 5.10).*

4. While there are prettier ways to turn a corner, the easiest way is to sew to the end of the appliqué, stopping with the needle on the outside edge. Pivot 90 degrees, lower the foot and continue sewing (Fig. 5.11). You may have to lengthen the stitch slightly at each corner so the foot feeds smoothly over the stitches in the corner.

SEW-HOW: *For a softer more pliable appliqué, thread your sewing machine with all-purpose sewing thread on top and fusible thread in the bobbin. Stitch the outline of the appliqué, cut it out very close to the stitching line, and fuse it onto the base fabric. Then satin stitch around the perimeter (see "Decorative Cords, Flosses, and Ribbons" in Chapter Four).*

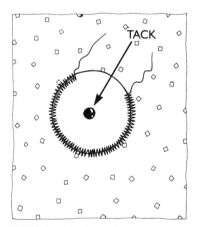

TACK

Fig. 5.10: *A thumb tack or circle-making accessory works like a center point in a compass so fabric feeds in a perfect circle and stitches fan out automatically.*

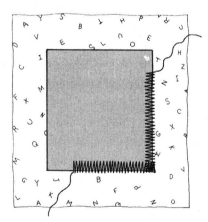

Fig. 5.11: *Turn a satin-stitched corner by sewing to the end of the appliqué, pivoting 90 degrees, and continue sewing.*

BEADS, BAUBLES, AND BANGLES

Many of us who sew collect fabric. We also collect thread, ribbon, floss, yarn, beads, and charms in case a future project calls for them. We find our collections are a great source of inspiration. Whenever possible, we dip into the inventory for texturing projects. Most buttons and beads can be attached by machine. Cross-locked sequins and beads can be applied with your sewing machine or serger. Here are the basics.

Attaching a Single Bead by Machine

Beads, charms and watch parts can be attached by machine if the hole in the bead or bauble is large enough and your needle fine enough. The thickness of the bead also matters. Before attaching, check that the needle can pass through the bead and that the needle clamp in its lowest position clears the bead.

Machine Readiness Checklist

- *Stitch:* zigzag
- *Foot:* none
- *Stitch length:* 0
- *Stitch width:* wide enough to clear the hole and the wall of the bead
- *Needle:* 60/9 to 70/10 universal
- *Needle position:* far left
- *Thread:* nylon monofilament or appropriate color
- *Feed dogs:* lowered
- *Miscellaneous:* glue stick

1. Dot the bead with glue stick and position it on the fabric.

2. Place the fabric under the needle, lower the presser bar lever, move the flywheel by hand, and take a stitch. Pull the bobbin thread up through the surface of the fabric and hold both top and bobbin threads to one side. Move the flywheel by hand, walking the needle back and forth so it clears the edge of the bead. Step on the foot pedal and stitch several zigzags until the bead is secure. Some machines can be programmed for a certain number of stitches, then lock off (check your Operating Manual).

3. Move the stitch width to zero and take a few stitches in place, outside the bead, to lock off.

4. Repeat for as many beads as needed. Attach a large bead by threading a cord through it and freely stitching it on either side (Fig. 5.12).

    VARIATION: *To attach an individual bead or charm to the edge or corners, Robbie Fanning uses water-soluble stabilizer in a hoop. Place the free fabric edge on the stabilizer and put the charm on the edge of the fabric. Zigzag on the fabric edge through the hole of the charm, then off onto the stabilizer several times to secure it. Finally, remove everything from the hoop, tie off the threads, tear off the stabilizer, then dissolve any stabilizer caught in the threads.*

A.

B.

C.

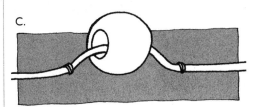

Fig. 5.12: *Glue-stick bead to the fabric; using a zigzag, walk needle back and forth from the center of the bead to the outside edge (a). Move width to zero to lock off the stitch. When needed, do the same thing on the opposite edge of the bead (b). Attach a large bead by threading a cord through it and freely stitching over cord on either side (c).*

Attaching a String of Beads by Machine

1. Set your machine as described in "Attaching a Single Bead by Machine." String beads onto a thread and lay them on a table or flat surface in front of the machine. Freely stitch one end of the beaded thread, attaching it to the fabric (see "Free-Machine Embroidery and Quilting" later in this chapter).

2. Stitch along the thread the width of one bead. Push the first bead near the anchored end.

3. Freely stitch along the length of another bead; push it up and stitch over the beaded thread. Repeat, pushing up and stitching from bead to bead until the string is attached (Fig. 5.13).

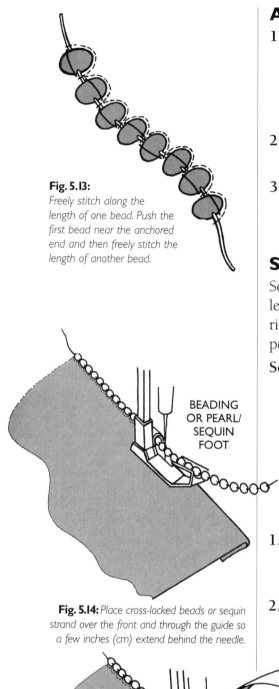

Fig. 5.13:
Freely stitch along the length of one bead. Push the first bead near the anchored end and then freely stitch the length of another bead.

Serging Cross-Locked Beads and Sequins

Serge over cross-locked glass beads (beads strung together on a length of thread and purchased by the yard through your local fabric or craft store) and sequins with your serger and the beading or pearl/sequin foot.

Serger Readiness Checklist

- *Stitch:* balanced three-thread
- *Foot:* beading or pearl/sequin
- *Stitch length:* as long as bead diameter
- *Stitch width:* as wide as the bead diameter
- *Needle:* appropriate for the fabric
- *Thread:* monofilament or all-purpose thread to match fabric
- *Miscellaneous:* cross-locking beads or sequins no larger than 4mm

1. Place the cross-locked beads or sequin strand over the front and through the guide of the foot so a few inches (cm) extend behind the needle (Fig. 5.14).

Fig. 5.14: *Place cross-locked beads or sequin strand over the front and through the guide so a few inches (cm) extend behind the needle.*

BEADING OR PEARL/ SEQUIN FOOT

2. Position the fabric under the foot so the beads are at the fold or edge of the seamline between the needle and knives. For a clean finish at a raw edge, plan to serge off the seam allowance as shown in Figure 5.15. Begin slowly serging, holding the bead or sequin tail and guiding the fabric so the beads/sequins peek out between the upper and lower looper threads. Add cross-locked beads to tucks, pocket flaps, cuffs, or front plackets.

SERGING SAVVY: You can also attach beads with the flat-lock and rolled edge stitches. Read more about it in Creative Serging Illustrated *by Pati Palmer, Gail Brown, and Sue Green, (Chilton, 1994).*

SEW HOW: To attach cross-locked beads with the sewing machine, couch over the beads with a zigzag stitch that is the width and length of an individual bead on the strand (see "Couching the Carefree Way" later in this chapter).

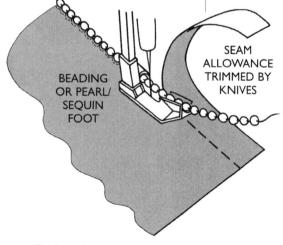

BEADING OR PEARL/ SEQUIN FOOT

SEAM ALLOWANCE TRIMMED BY KNIVES

Fig. 5.15: *For a clean finish, serge off the seam allowances.*

BLOOMING FABRIC

1. Cut, layer, stack, and pin together three 12" (30.5cm) squares of coordinating fabrics (Fig. 5.16). Cut the fourth 12" (30.5cm) square and set it aside (for this, we fused lamé with interfacing to prevent raveling and to add stability) (Fig. 5.17). If you want to use another fabric, choose your highest contrast (lightest or darkest) fabric for this layer.

2. Mark the square on the straight and cross grain as shown (Fig. 5.18a). Set the machine for straight quilting (see "Straight Quilting" later in this chapter). Move the quilting bar out so it guides 1" (2.5cm) from the needle. Starting in the middle, quilt out to the sides of the square (Fig. 5.18b) in both directions.

3. Using the rotary cutter and mat, cut across each 1" (2.5cm) square by rolling the cutter from one corner to the other, cutting the square on the bias (Fig. 5.19). Then go back and use the sharp embroidery or appliqué scissors and clip up to but *not through* the stitches (this is an easy step to complete while watching TV with the family).

4. Once all squares are cut in both directions, pin cut square over fourth 12" (30.5cm) square, and requilt over original stitching lines (Fig. 5.20). This is a great place to use one of your decorative machine stitches.

5. Wet this square and toss it in the dryer with a clean tennis ball or tennis shoe and completely dry the square. Because the quilted squares are cut on the bias, the fabric will bloom without raveling.

BOBBIN WORK THAT'S ALMOST PLAY

This technique is loads of fun. You sew with the fabric upside down and don't know how your work looks until you turn it over. (Always sew a sample first, using the same fabric, stabilizer, and threads you'll use in the finished piece, adjusting tensions as needed.)

Machine Readiness Checklist
- *Stitch:* straight, zigzag, open decorative (i.e., feather, scallop, wave)
- *Foot:* embroidery/appliqué
- *Stitch length:* appropriate for stitch
- *Stitch width:* 0; 3–5
- *Needle:* appropriate for fabric
- *Thread:* monofilament in top; pearl cotton, embroidery floss, ribbon floss, or silk or acrylic ribbon in bobbin
- *Tension:* tighten top slightly; make bobbin very loose or bypass it (see your Operating Manual)

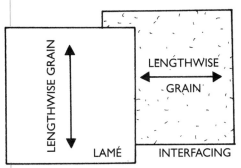

Fig. 5.16: *Stack two or three layers of fabric.*

Fig. 5.17: *Fuse lamé with interfacing so the grains are opposite one another, then set this fourth square aside.*

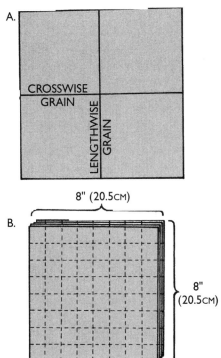

Fig. 5.18: *Mark lines down the center of the layered square both on the crosswise and lengthwise grain (a). Using your quilt bar, straight quilt the layered square every inch [2.5cm] (b).*

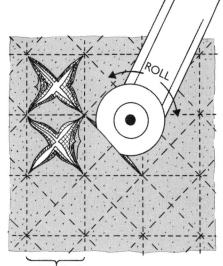

Fig. 5.19: *Rock your rotary cutter across each square from corner to corner.*

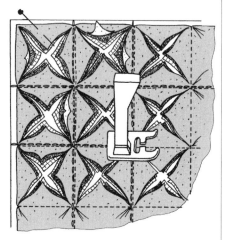

Fig. 5.20: *Lay cut layers over bottom square and requilt over the original stitching lines.*

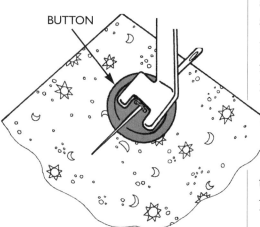

BUTTON

Fig. 5.21: *Use a tapestry needle between the holes of the button-sewing foot to make a button shank.*

Stabilizer: fusible interfacing or tear-away (you won't need a stabilizer if your fabric is in a hoop or mounted on a foundation or batting)

This is one technique we like to test before adding to a piece because the weight of the fabric and the decorative fiber will influence the creative process. You should also take into account whether the fabric has been scrunched (see p. 76) or is smooth all over.

1. Wind a bobbin with decorative thread and thread it in your bobbin case. Loosen your bobbin tension so it pulls smoothly. You may want to bypass the tension altogether (see your Operating Manual).

   SEW-HOW: *We use separate bobbin cases for our texturing projects — one for regular sewing, and one marked with nail polish for experimenting.*

2. Pull up the bobbin thread as normal, then place the fabric right-side-down against the feed dogs and sew. While testing, experiment with several stitches. Bobbin work can also be done freely using a darning foot on the machine (see "Free-Machine Embroidery and Quilting" later in this chapter).

BUTTON SEWING — BUT NOT BY HAND

We added buttons to many of the textures in this book for color, dimension, and interest. Once your machine is threaded, you can stitch on a row of buttons in minutes using your button sewing foot, a glue stick and a little liquid seam sealant. While the foot is not always necessary, it's a lot easier and is often included as a standard accessory—so let's get it out and use it.

Its short toes are sometimes covered with a rubber sleeve, or it may have a grip on the underside so the button will not slip. Some feet are transparent for good visibility; most have a narrow channel underneath to hold a heavy needle, or have an adjustable shank-maker used to create a thread shank (Fig. 5.21). Look how designer Linnette Whicker used buttons to add dimension to her "Hearts and Flowers" in the Designer Showcase in the color pages.

Machine Readiness Checklist

- *Stitch:* zigzag or button-sewing
- *Foot:* button-sewing, standard zigzag, or none
- *Stitch length:* 0 or drop feed dogs
- *Stitch width:* 3-4 (wide enough to clear the holes)
- *Needle:* appropriate for the fabric
- *Thread:* all-purpose sewing thread

Tension: loosen top slightly; bobbin, normal

Stabilizer: none

Accessories: tapestry needle (optional, used under foot to create space between the button and fabric for a shank)

1. Mark the button placement with a disappearing marker.

2. Dot the back of the button with the glue stick, then stick the button onto the fabric.

3. Set your machine in far-left needle position. Newer models may have the special button-sewing stitch available (see your Operating Manual). Place the project under the needle, turn your flywheel by hand so the needle stops in the left hole of the button, then lower the presser foot onto the button.

4. Again, turn the flywheel by hand to check the needle clearance; adjust your zigzag width if necessary, then stitch several zigzag stitches to secure the button. Move the stitch width to zero and take a few stitches in place to anchor the threads (some newer models have an automatic lock-off; see your Operating Manual). Remove the fabric from under the foot and pull off enough thread to wrap a shank between the button and fabric (Fig. 5.22).

5. After wrapping the shank, pull threads to the back, tie, and clip them off at the fabric. Dot knotted threads with liquid seam sealant. Buttons sewn on this way should stay on for the life of the garment.

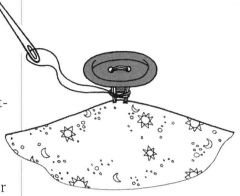

Fig. 5.22: *Remove the fabric from under the foot and pull off enough thread to wrap a shank between the button and fabric.*

COUCHING THE CAREFREE WAY

Couching means to attach a fiber on the surface fabric at certain intervals. To create dimension, couch over fiber, beads, sequins, yarn, ribbon, pulled threads, cord, gimp, cordonnet—get the picture? Look at how designer Diana Cedolia couches over decorative cord on the textured piece Just Doodling Around (see the Designer Showcase in the color pages).

Machine Readiness Checklist

- *Stitch:* straight; zigzag
- *Foot:* braiding, cording, and/or piping foot (depending on the thickness of the cord)
- *Stitch length:* 1-2.5 (13-24 stitches per inch) for small curves; 3-4 (6-9 stitches per inch) for large curves
- *Stitch width:* 0-wide enough to clear the cord on either side
- *Needle:* appropriate for the fabric
- *Thread:* nylon monofilament or all-purpose sewing thread to match cord
- *Tension:* normal

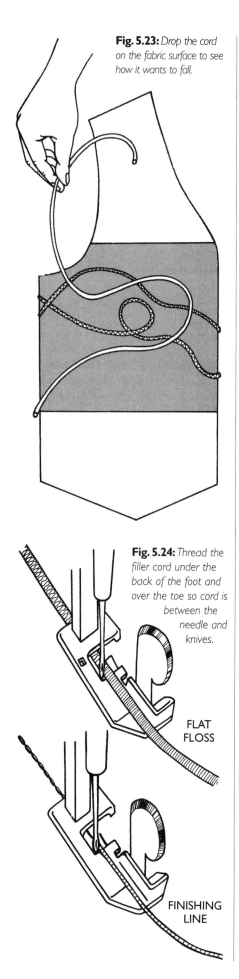

Fig. 5.23: *Drop the cord on the fabric surface to see how it wants to fall.*

Fig. 5.24: *Thread the filler cord under the back of the foot and over the toe so cord is between the needle and knives.*

FLAT FLOSS

FINISHING LINE

Stabilizer: use as needed; fabric may only need to be starched

Accessories: ribbon or sequin guide (if you are using flat ribbon, braid, or baby rickrack)

Miscellaneous: glue stick, disappearing marker

1. Arrange the cord on the fabric in a pleasing way. We often place the fabric on a flat surface and then drop the cord to see how it wants to fall (Fig. 5.23). Mark the line with your marker.

2. Once you have decided where you want the cord, thread it through the foot and ribbon guide; stitch it to the surface of the fabric.

   SEW-HOW: *If you don't have a braiding, piping, or cording foot, dot glue stick on the back of the cord and glue-baste cord in place. Using the embroidery foot, stitch the cord to the base fabric.*

Making Wide Serger Braid

If you can't find the cord you need to couch over for a specific effect, serge it.

Serger Readiness Checklist

- *Stitch:* wide balanced three-thread stitch
- *Foot:* standard
- *Stitch length:* 2-3
- *Stitch width:* wide
- *Needle:* left, 80/12 universal
- *Thread:* all-purpose sewing thread in the needle; #8 pearl cotton or Decor 6 in the upper looper; all-purpose sewing thread, fusible thread, or Decor 6 in the lower looper
- *Tension:* balanced so the decorative thread lies flat on the filler (you may have to loosen your tension on upper and lower loopers threaded with decorative threads—always test first)
- *Stabilizer/filler cord:* ribbon floss, Seams Great (narrow tricot cut across the grain available on a roll from your local sewing machine, fabric, or mail-order source); pearl cotton; ribbon floss; narrow elastic braid

Thread the filler cord over the toe and under the back of the foot so it is between the needle and the knives; then serge. Stitches should lay smoothly over the filler cord, locking on either side (Fig. 5.24). When you apply serger braid with your sewing machine, you'll find it is easy to turn curves and corners because the serged stitches can be moved along the filler cord to fan around a curve (Fig. 5.25).

SERGING SAVVY: *For an even easier braid application, use fusible thread in the lower looper. This thread has a fusing agent in it that melts when pressed so the serged braid adheres to the fabric. After fusing to the fabric, couch the serger braid to the fabric using a straight or zigzag stitch.*

Making Narrow Serger Cord

Serger Readiness Checklist

- *Stitch:* narrow rolled hem
- *Foot:* rolled hem
- *Stitch length:* short (rolled hem setting, see your Operating Manual)
- *Stitch width:* narrow
- *Needle:* right for rolled hem; 90/14 stretch or 100/16 universal
- *Thread:* all-purpose sewing thread in the needle; decorative metallic thread such as Madeira "Glamour" in the upper and lower loopers
- *Tension:* rolled hem (see your Operating Manual)
- *Stabilizer:* none

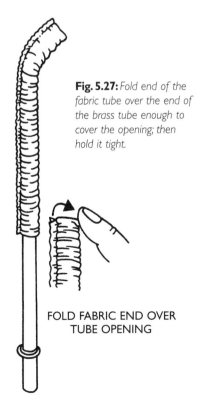

1. Make rolled-hem chain by holding the threads behind the foot and gently pulling on them while serging. Then couch this narrow braid onto a base fabric (see "Couching the Carefree Way" earlier in this chapter). Look for designer Patsy Shields' "Glamour Vest" featured in the Designer Showcase (see the color pages).

2. You may also create narrow serger braid by using rayon thread on the needle and upper and lower loopers, then serging over four-to-twenty-pound-test fish line. Set your serger for the narrow rolled edge and guide the fish line between the needle and knives. The fish line becomes the filler thread, adding dimension to the narrow braid.

SERGING SAVVY: *Some serger models allow for a two-thread rolled hem which produces a soft edge because there is less thread in the stitch. Check your Operating Manual to see if your model has this capability.*

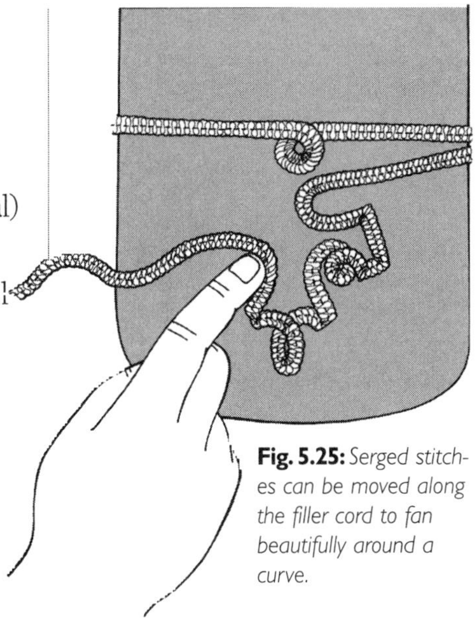

Fig. 5.25: *Serged stitches can be moved along the filler cord to fan beautifully around a curve.*

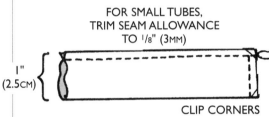

FOR SMALL TUBES, TRIM SEAM ALLOWANCE TO 1/8" (3MM)

1" (2.5CM)

CLIP CORNERS

Fig. 5.26: *Fold the fabric strip in half the long way and stitch a 1/4" (3mm) seam the length of the tube and across one end. Ends may be left open if a finished end is not needed.*

FABRIC TUBES MADE FAST AND FUN

Have you avoided making spaghetti straps or fabric button loops because you didn't like to turn them? Learn these two easy ways and use tubes as another texturing medium. Designer Sandra Benfield couched tubes over a scrunched foundation using decorative machine stitches to keep them in place in her "Fastube Texture" (see the Designer Showcase in the color pages).

Fasturn Fabric Tubes

Fasturn—a collection of different-sized tubes and hooks available at sewing and craft shops—makes fast work of fabric tubes.

1. Cut fabric strips twice the width needed, plus 1/2" (1.3cm) for seam allowances. For example, for a 1" (2.5cm) flat finished tube, cut your fabric strip the desired length and 2-1/2" (6.5cm) wide.

Fig. 5.27: *Fold end of the fabric tube over the end of the brass tube enough to cover the opening; then hold it tight.*

FOLD FABRIC END OVER TUBE OPENING

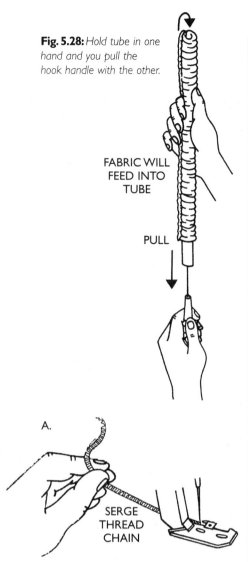

Fig. 5.28: *Hold tube in one hand and you pull the hook handle with the other.*

FABRIC WILL FEED INTO TUBE

PULL

A.

SERGE THREAD CHAIN

Fig. 5.29: *Serge a thread chain longer than finished tube. Encase chain, then serge along the length of the tube, careful that chain inside tube is against the fold.*

B.

SERGE SEAM

C.

PULL END OF CHAIN TO TURN

SEW-HOW: *For tubes that can be shaped into curves, cut the fabric on the bias and sew the seam using a one-width, one-length (24 stitches per inch) zigzag.*

2. Fold the fabric strip in half the long way, right sides together and stitch a ¹/₄" (3mm) seam the length of the tube and across one end (Fig. 5.26). Ends may be left open if a finished end is not needed.

3. Slip the fabric tube over the long brass tube until the closed end of the fabric tube is tight against the brass tube. If the end of the tube is open, fold the end of the fabric tube over the end of the brass tube just enough to cover the opening; then hold it tight Fig. 5.27).

4. Insert the hook into the brass tube from the open handle-end. Holding the fabric taut over the end of the tube, push the hook point through the fabric while twisting the hook to the right until the entire hook is through.

5. Holding the tube with one hand, ease the fabric toward the turning end. As you begin pulling the hook handle with the other hand, pull the wire straight out of the tube (Fig. 5.28). Remove the hook by untwisting the end. When you buy a Fasturn, a detailed instruction manual with several fool-proof tips and suggestions for use comes with it. You can also register your Fasturn set and receive periodic newsletters and product updates.

Serger-Turned Fabric Tubes

1. Cut your fabric strip the desired width, allowing ¹/₂" (1.3cm) for seam allowances. Set your serger for a short narrow balanced three-thread overlock stitch and serge a thread chain longer than the finished tube (Fig. 5.29a). Don't cut off the chain.

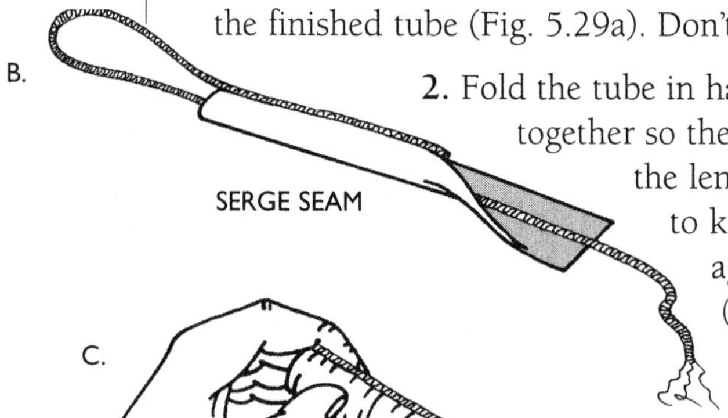

2. Fold the tube in half the long way right sides together so the chain is encased. Serge along the length of the tube, being careful to keep the chain inside and against the fold of the tube (Fig. 5.29b).

3. Gently pull the chain to turn the tube (Fig. 5.29c).

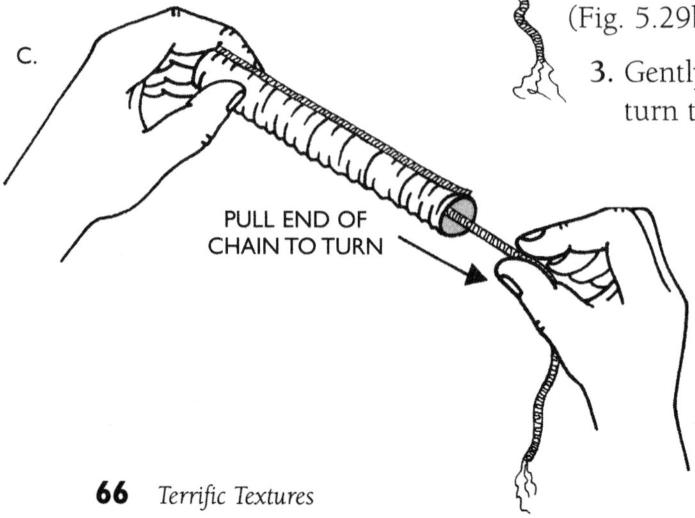

FLATLOCKING MOST FABULOUS

For a decorative topstitch, flatlock the edge of a free-flowing appliqué or tuck. For a sashiko-look to the ladder side of the flatlock, thread your needle with cordonnet or topstitching thread (see "Sashiko Secrets" later in this chapter).

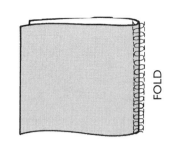

Two-Thread Flatlock

Some sergers can use two threads to stitch a flatlock (check your Operating Manual). To do this, thread one needle and one looper for a two-thread overedge. Set for a balanced stitch and serge along the cut or folded edge. Because the two-thread overedge doesn't lock at the seamline, the flatlock automatically opens when you pull it flat.

Three-Thread Flatlock

For the widest flatlock, thread the left needle and both loopers; set stitch length for a short- to medium-width stitch. Loosen the needle tension almost to zero, and tighten the lower looper until the thread forms a straight line on the right side of the stitch. Guide the fabric fold or cut edges so the fabric fills half the width of the stitch (Fig. 5.30).

Fig. 5.30: *Guide the fabric fold or cut edges so the fabric fills half the stitch.*

FREE-MACHINE EMBROIDERY AND QUILTING

Free-machine embroidery and quilting means that the feed dogs are covered or lowered and the fabric is moved freely under the needle while sewing. This is often done on a piece of fabric using a straight, zigzag, or decorative stitch. It is also often done to freely quilt around a center medallion or to stipple an area in machine quilting (Fig. 5.32; see *The Complete Book of Machine Quilting, Second Edition* by Robbie and Tony Fanning, Chilton, 1994).

Machine Readiness Checklist

	Quilting and Stippling	*Zigzag Outline and Filling-In*
• *Stitch:*	straight	zigzag
• *Foot:*	none or darning	same
• *Stitch length:*	0	same
• *Stitch width:*	0	2-5
• *Needle:*	90/14 quilting, jeans, or stretch	same
• *Thread:*	appropriate for the project	same
• *Tension:*	normal	loosened slightly
• *Stabilizer:*	quilt batting	tear-away or iron-on tear-away (optional)
• *Accessories:*	embroidery hoop (optional)	embroidery hoop (optional)

Fig. 5.31: *Quilt around a center medallion or to stipple/granite stitch an area.*

Fig. 5.32: *A popular stippling or quilting texture we call the "granite stitch," looks like random curves and loops.*

1. Place your fabric in an embroidery hoop and pull the edges taut so when you tap the surface it sounds like a drum. Note that you put the fabric in a hoop for machine embroidery and quilting so that the larger ring is *under* the fabric and the smaller ring is *on top* of the fabric, just the opposite of hand embroidery and quilting.

2. Place your work under the needle, lower the presser bar (this engages your upper tension even though you don't have a presser foot on the machine). Holding the needle thread in your left hand, turn the flywheel with your right hand and complete a stitch; bring the bobbin thread up through the surface of the fabric.

3. Take several locking stitches in one place; then begin stitching quickly while moving the fabric slowly, and travel across the fabric to outline a center quilt medallion or to embroider a flower. Stop, then clip the beginning thread ends at the fabric.

SEW-HOW: *A popular stippling or quilting texture we call the granite stitch looks like random curves and loops. (We used it on the Scrap-Saver's Removable Yoke and the Warp-and-Woof Wear projects in Chapter Two.) Use the free-machine-embroidery method to make granite stitches in whatever size you need; use the programmed version of the stitch available on some machines for a finer, more precise look.*

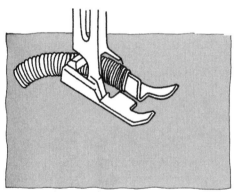

Fig. 5.33: *Zigzag over the fringe foot with a loosened satin stitch.*

Fig. 5.34: *Thread stands away from the fabric creating three-dimensional texture to make a rainbow, flower, grass, or eyelashes.*

FRINGED FLOWER CENTERS

FRINGING FUN AND FROLIC

Make fringe as fine as eyelashes or as heavy as doll hair using two very different techniques.

Fringe Foot Frivolity

This fun foot is sometimes called a looping, tailor tacking, or special marking foot and has one or two blades that stick up off the surface of the fabric. When used with the zigzag stitch, the blade causes the thread to stand away from the fabric. While it was initially invented for making tailor tacks to mark a pattern, we like it better for its texturing capabilities to make chenille, fringe for flowers, eyelashes, grass, or to add dimension to a flat surface. A good example is designer Marilyn Gatz's circle of fringe in "Hodge-Podge Excitement," found in the Designer Showcase in the color pages.

Machine Readiness Checklist

- *Stitch:* zigzag
- *Foot:* fringe
- *Stitch length:* 0.5-0.8 (60 stitches per inch or finer)
- *Stitch width:* 4-4.5
- *Needle:* 90/14 embroidery, jeans, or stretch
- *Thread:* rayon embroidery thread (if you thread two or three threads through the same needle to fill in faster or to thread-blend, you may have to lengthen the stitch to 0.8)

- *Tension:* loosened on top so fringe stands up on the fabric; bobbin, normal
- *Stabilizer:* tear-away or iron-on tear-away
- *Accessories:* the Thread Palette for using two to four threads simultaneously

Decide where you want the fringe, set your machine as described above and sew (Fig. 5.33). Make a sampler using different threads and blending threads. Try both wide and narrow stitches. To make a circle or square, start in the center and work out (Fig. 5.34).

Fringe Fork Follies

When you can't find purchased fringe, make your own. Wrap yarn, cord, soutache, ribbon, floss, gimp, rattail, serger braid, and chenille singly or together over a fringe fork to create custom fringe for any surface or seam.

Machine Readiness Checklist

- *Stitch:* straight or zigzag
- *Foot:* embroidery/appliqué
- *Stitch length:* 3-4 (6-9 stitches per inch)
- *Stitch width:* 0
- *Needle:* 90/14 jeans
- *Thread:* all-purpose sewing thread
- *Tension:* normal
- *Stabilizer:* adding machine tape
- *Accessories:* carpet fork or weaver's reed (available through your local sewing machine dealer), hairpin lace loom (available at craft stores), or fringe fork (available from Sew Art International; see Sources of Supplies at the back of the book)

SEW-HOW: *If you don't have one of the fringe-making accessories above, make one by bending a wire hanger the width you need. To make a separator to keep prongs rigid while wrapping them with yarn, cut and attach a length of the hanger protector cardboard (Fig. 5.35). Remove separator before sewing.*

1. Wrap the fork with yarn or any of the previously mentioned fibers. We like to use at least three colors or textures for our fringe.

2. Place the fringe and adding machine tape under the foot so the tape is against the feed dogs. Sew down one side or in the middle of the loops to attach the fringe to the tape. The tape prevents the fringe from curling so it is easier to apply.

3. Leave the adding machine tape on to attach the fringe to the fabric. The needle perforates the paper so it falls away after application (Fig. 5.36).

Texas Mink Fringe

1. Pre-shrink and cut strips of up to four different fabrics on the

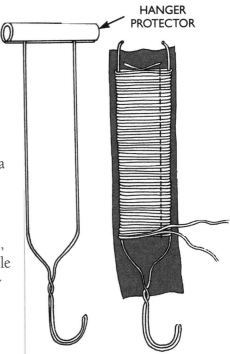

Fig. 5.35: *To keep prongs rigid while wrapping yarn or cord, cut and attach a length of the hanger-protector cardboard to make a separator.*

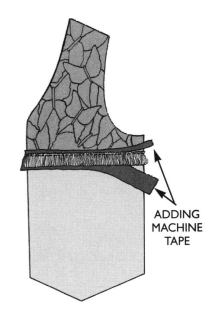

Fig. 5.36: *Stitch fringe to adding machine tape so it won't twist. Then apply to the project, adding machine tape and all. The needle perforates the paper so it falls away after application.*

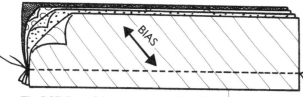

Fig. 5.37: *Stack fabric strips so the right side of one strip is against the wrong side of another.*

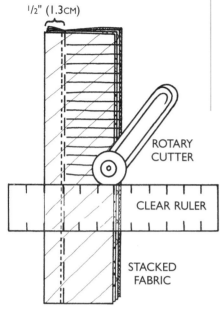

1/2" (1.3CM)

ROTARY CUTTER

CLEAR RULER

STACKED FABRIC

Fig. 5.38: *Stitch fabric strips together 1/2" (1.3cm) from the edge. Cut 1/2" (1.3cm) wide fringe stopping the cut 1/8" (3mm) from the stitching line. Wet fringe strip and toss in the dryer. Because it is cut on the bias, it won't ravel.*

bias, the width of the fringe you want plus 5/8" (1.5cm) for the seam allowance. Stack strips so the right side of one is against the wrong side of the other (Fig. 5.37).

2. Stitch the stack together on one side, sewing 1/2" (1.3cm) from the cut edge.

3. Lay the fringe strip on your cutting mat. Using a clear ruler and rotary cutter, begin cutting 1/2" (1.3cm) fringe, stopping the cut 1/8" (3mm) from the stitching line (Fig. 5.38).

4. Wet fringe strip and toss in the dryer with a clean tennis ball or tennis shoe until the strip is dry. Because the fringe is cut on the bias it won't ravel, and the fringe curls will create a wonderful texture (Fig. 5.39).

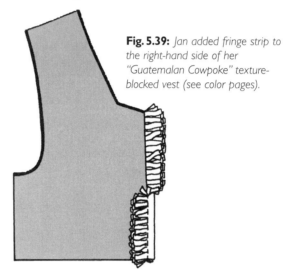

Fig. 5.39: *Jan added fringe strip to the right-hand side of her "Guatemalan Cowpoke" texture-blocked vest (see color pages).*

PIPING UP FOR TEXTURE

Piping can be purchased or made from your own fabric. The filler cord, called cable cord, is round and twisted and comes in widths from 1/8" to 1/2" (3mm-1.3cm). The cord can be a shiny rayon, spun satiny rayon, cotton, or combed fibers, each creating a unique texture.

1. To cover cable cord with fabric, use bias-cut fabric strips cut the circumference of the cord plus 1/2" (1.3cm) for seam allowances. For thicker cord add 1" (2.5cm) for 1/2" (1.3cm) seam allowances. Sandwich cable cord inside the fabric strip and use either your zipper or piping foot to stitch cord into the fabric (Fig. 5.40).

SEW-HOW: *Fabric-covered cord is also available by the yard and found prepackaged or on a bolt in the trim area of your local fabric store. For straight applications, the piping you make and cover yourself can be cut across the grain to save on fabric. If piping will go around a curve, the fabric that covers the cable cord should be cut on the bias.*

2. Attach the piping to the right side of your project using the piping foot on your sewing machine or serger.

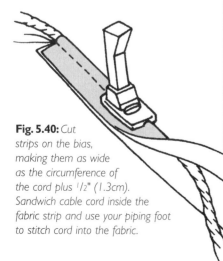

Fig. 5.40: *Cut strips on the bias, making them as wide as the circumference of the cord plus 1/2" (1.3cm). Sandwich cable cord inside the fabric strip and use your piping foot to stitch cord into the fabric.*

3. At a corner, clip piping seam allowance to the stitching, without cutting through the cord. With the needle in the fabric, raise the foot and pivot. Nudge your index finger into the corner so the cord bends around your finger and is away from the needle. Lower the presser foot and stitch (Fig. 5.41).

4. When you get to the join, overlap and butt cord ends and fold the fabric into the piping as shown (Fig. 5.42).

5. Place fabric, right sides together, so the stitching from the previous step is where you can see it.

6. Decenter the needle on your sewing machine so it falls between the previous row of stitching and the bump of the piping. This way you're sewing closer to the cord so you don't see the previous row of stitching when the project is turned right side out (Fig. 5.43).

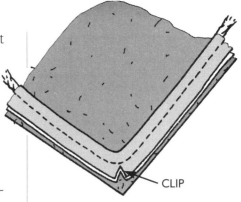

CLIP

Fig. 5.41: *Attach piping to the right side of your project using a piping foot on your sewing machine or serger. For smooth corners, clip piping seam allowance almost to the stitching line and nudge your finger into the corner so the piping bends around your finger.*

CUT CORD AND BUTT ENDS

Fig. 5.42: *Decenter the needle so it falls between the previous row of stitching and the bump of the piping. Overlap and butt cord ends at the join.*

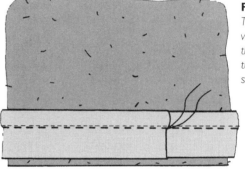

FOLD AND OVERLAP

Fig. 5.43: *The cord isn't visible when the project is turned right side out.*

QUILTING QUIPS

Machine quilting is a much larger topic than we have room to cover here so we recommend you look in the beginning of our book for the list of Chilton's quilting books—they're sure to spark your interest. Also look for *The Complete Book of Machine Quilting, Second Edition,* by Robbie and Tony Fanning, Chilton, 1994, for even more inspiration. For the texturing ideas in this book, you only need the following machine-quilting basics. (Also see "Free-Machine Embroidery and Quilting" earlier in this chapter and "Sashiko Secrets" and "Most-Excellent Echo-Quilting" later in this chapter.)

Serged Piecing

Piecing can be done quickly and easily on your serger. To keep as little thread in the seams as possible, use a two-ply serger thread and a balanced three-thread overlock stitch. Remember to test for best results. For exact 1/4" (6mm) seams, you may have to adjust the stitch width (Fig. 5.44).

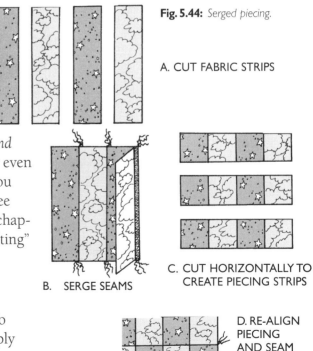

Fig. 5.44: *Serged piecing.*

A. CUT FABRIC STRIPS

B. SERGE SEAMS

C. CUT HORIZONTALLY TO CREATE PIECING STRIPS

D. RE-ALIGN PIECING AND SEAM

Straight Quilting

Machine Readiness Checklist

- *Stitch:* straight
- *Foot:* walking, embroidery/appliqué, or extra-wide embroidery foot used for large embroidery motifs
- *Stitch length:* 3-4 (6-9 stitches per inch)
- *Stitch width:* 0
- *Needle:* 75/11 or 90/14 quilting
- *Thread:* all-purpose sewing thread
- *Tension:* normal
- *Pressure:* normal to slightly lighter than normal
- *Stabilizer:* batting
- *Accessories:* quilting bar (optional)
- *Miscellaneous:* safety pins for basting

Make your quilt sandwich—top, batting, and backing—pin it together and quilt row after row, starting in the center of the piece and quilting out to the edges. If the quilt sandwich is well-pinned, you can start quilting anywhere. You may want to practice this on a scrap first.

> **SEW-HOW:** *A walking foot with a quilting bar attached can be very useful. The walking foot prevents fabric distortion while keeping the under layer from coming up short. The quilting bar keeps you guiding straight.*

If you don't have a walking foot, try one of these variations.

- Use the embroidery or roller foot with the quilting bar, usually standard equipment, for straight quilting. Place the bar on your machine as described in your Operating Manual and move it out the distance desired. This guide helps keep your quilting rows straight and an even distance from each other. The roller foot has feed dog-like rollers that help to feed the top fabric layer evenly to the backing.

- Some machines make extra-large embroidery designs and use a special foot for this. If you have this extra-wide embroidery foot, you can use it with your quilting bar for straight quilting. The larger foot displaces more pressure over a larger area for better results.

- For an interesting variation on straight quilting, use open decorative stitches to quilt the rows. Many machines have scallop, wave, three-step zigzag, multiple zigzag, or feather stitches that work great for your quilted texturing projects (Fig. 5.45).

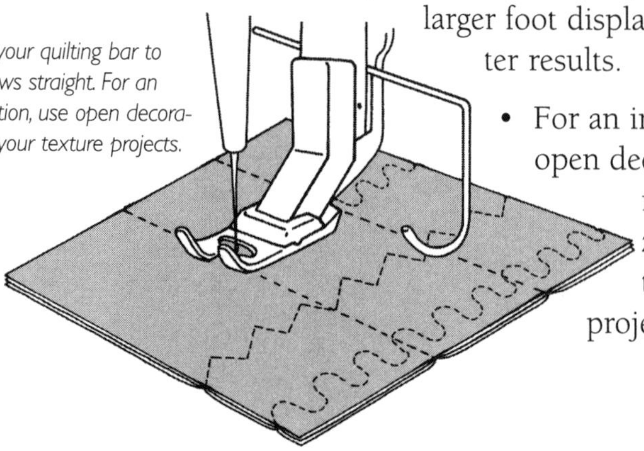

Fig. 5.45: *Use your quilting bar to guide quilting rows straight. For an interesting variation, use open decorative stitches for your texture projects.*

SASHIKO SECRETS

According to Saikoh Takano, author of *Sashiko and Beyond* (Chilton, 1992), "The Japanese word *sashiko* means 'little stabs,' or running stitch. Originally this simple hand stitch was used as a practical technique to quilt together several layers of loosely woven fabric for strength and warmth." Sashiko coats were worn by fire fighters as protective clothing when drenched with water; the decorative side was worn in. This beautiful quilting technique is used today in quilts, wearable art clothing, and is easy to simulate by machine. You can even create a serged sashiko stitch with a narrow flatlock using a cordonnet or topstitching thread through the needle (see "Flatlocking Most Fabulous" earlier in this chapter).

Machine Readiness Checklist

- *Stitch:* straight
- *Foot:* embroidery/appliqué
- *Stitch length:* 3-3.5 (6-8 stitches per inch)
- *Stitch width:* 0
- *Needle:* 90/14–100/16 jeans, topstitch, or 120/20 universal for heavier rayon threads such as Madeira's Decor or YLT's Designer 6
- *Thread:* white, ivory, or ecru cordonnet or topstitching thread, or rayon Decor or Designer 6 in top; black or navy all-purpose sewing thread in bobbin
- *Tension:* tighten top; loosen bobbin slightly so the dark knot shows on the right side of the fabric
- *Stabilizer:* water-soluble
- *Miscellaneous:* pre-shrunk lightweight denim or polished cotton ironed to cotton flannel for fabric and foundation, Sharpie marker or Pigma pen, water and spritzer

1. Place the denim or polished cotton and flannel wrong sides together and iron them from the center out (Fig. 5.46). The fuzz from the flannel sticks to the top fabric so the layers don't shift.

2. Stitch around the perimeter of the piece to hold the fabrics together.

3. Transfer the sashiko design in Figure 5.47 (or the design of your choice) onto a piece of water-soluble stabilizer (see Transferring Designs with Ease later in this chapter), and pin to the right side of the top fabric. For inspiration, read *Sashiko and Beyond,* or create your own designs.

4. Working from the center of the piece out, stitch over the design lines, pivoting as needed (Fig. 5.47). Rather than backstitching, we prefer pulling threads to the back and tying them off. Spritz your piece with water to remove the stabilizer.

SEW-HOW: *For smaller areas it may be necessary to put the fabric (top, foundation, and stabilizer) into an embroidery hoop.*

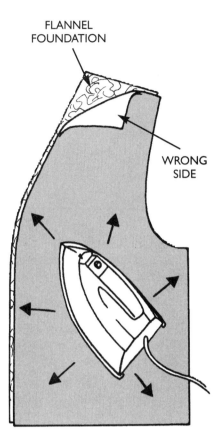

Fig. 5.46: *Place denim or polished cotton and flannel wrong sides together and iron them from the center out. The fuzz from the flannel sticks to the top fabric so the layers don't shift.*

Fig. 5.47: *Working from the center out, stitch over design lines, pivoting as needed.*

SATIN STITCHING FOR ALL REASONS

Satin stitching offers a myriad of decorating possibilities. Look at how designer Susan Rock used decorative machine stitches to attach woven ribbon to a printed foundation on Stripe-Easy-Stitch Wander in the Designer Showcase in the color pages. Satin stitches are also used at the edges of fused appliqués. Here we give tips on satin and decorative stitching, as well as directions for satin-stitched blobs, satin-stitched reverse Mola, "satin serging", and creating a "satin-serged" narrow rolled edge.

Satin and Decorative Stitch Strategy

For the best looking decorative and satin stitches, loosen your upper tension so stitches lock under the fabric and use:

- a good quality all-cotton, rayon, acrylic, or metallic machine embroidery thread

- a new size 90/14 embroidery, stretch, or jeans needle

- a basting or darning thread in your bobbin

- a stabilizer under your work

Satin-Stitched "Blobs"

We use satin-stitched blobs to fill in areas with dimensional texture. To do this, set your machine for a two- to six-width zigzag stitch and stitch several stitches in one place so they pile up on each other. Remember to move the width to zero and lock off each blob before proceeding to the next (Fig. 5.48). Some machines can be programmed so each blob is stitched the same number of zigzags then automatically locks off (see your Operating Manual). If you don't have this function, count the stitches instead.

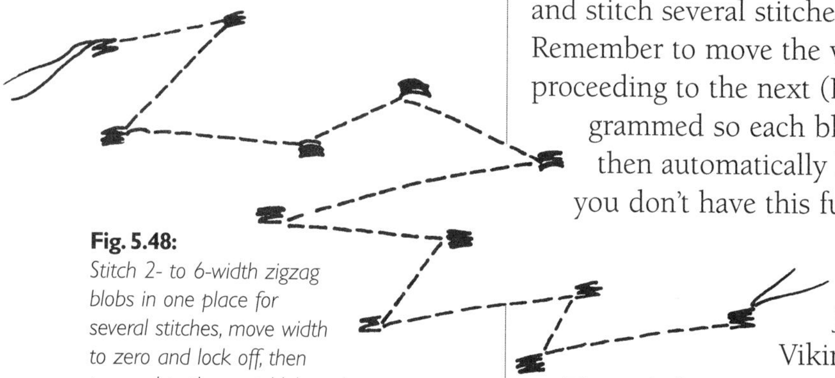

Fig. 5.48:
Stitch 2- to 6-width zigzag blobs in one place for several stitches, move width to zero and lock off, then proceed to the next blob and repeat.

Satin-Stitched Reverse Mola

Jan developed this technique for the Very Viking Vest contest, and her vest is shown in a Vogue/Viking pattern as well as in the Spring 1994 issue of *Vogue Patterns* magazine (see color pages). She has always admired the colorful reverse-embroidered molas, but never had the time to perfect the traditional skill of cutting away the top fabrics, and turning them under. Reverse mola is created by tapered satin stitches sewn on top of a black background.

Machine Readiness Checklist
- *Stitch:* tapered satin
- *Foot:* embroidery/appliqué
- *Stitch length:* 0.3-0.5 (60 stitches per inch)
- *Stitch width:* 0-6-0
- *Needle:* 90/14 stretch or jeans

- *Thread:* two rayon embroidery threads of the same color in top; black all-purpose sewing thread in bobbin
- *Tension:* loosen top slightly; bobbin, normal
- *Stabilizer:* pre-shrunk cotton flannel
- *Miscellaneous:* black woven cotton such as broadcloth or kettle cloth, disappearing chalk, clear plastic ruler, mola design

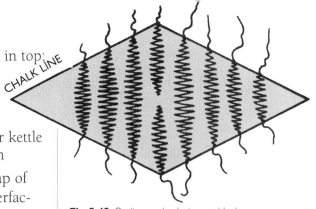

Fig. 5.49: *Outline mola design on black fabric using a disappearing chalk. Starting at the chalk line, taper the satin stitch out the desired width; stitch the bar as long as needed, then taper back to 0. Some machines have satin stitch motifs that can be programmed in to make the ends of each bar more uniform.*

1. Iron cotton flannel to the underside of black fabric. The nap of the flannel sticks to the black fabric almost like fusible interfacing, but is much softer. Draw an outline of the design on the black fabric to create the boundaries of the design.

2. Starting at the edge of the chalk boundary and with your stitch width at zero, taper the satin stitch out to about a five to six width. Stitch the bar as long as needed, then taper back to zero (see Fig. 5.49)

    SEW-HOW: *If you can program in or select a satin element or motif that looks like a rounded triangle, stitch it before the long line of satin stitching for more uniformity to the bars. Then program the same motif and flip it over to finish the bar.*

3. Add some sashiko stitching, then echo-quilt around the shapes to texture the rest of the fabric (see "Sashiko Secrets" earlier in this chapter and "Twin-Needle Texturing" later in this chapter).

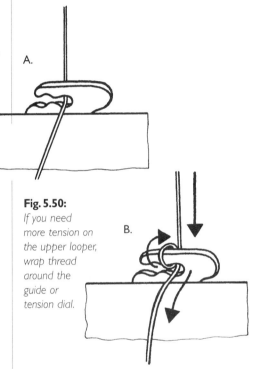

Fig. 5.50:
If you need more tension on the upper looper, wrap thread around the guide or tension dial.

A.

B.

"Satin Serging" Strategy

For the best looking decorative serged edges, try the following:

- Use decorative thread in the upper looper and all-purpose serger thread in the needle and lower looper. To make the edge fusible, use fusible thread in the lower looper.

- For a decorative stitch that looks great on both sides, use all-purpose serger thread in the needle and thread both the upper and lower loopers with the same decorative cord or floss.

- If the thread is heavy, stretchy, or has textural resistance (such as metallics, and pearl cotton), you may have to loosen the tension.

- If the thread is fine and slippery (such as rayons, nylons, and acrylics), you may have to tighten the tension for the desired results.

- If after using the tightest tension setting, you find you need even tighter tension (e.g., for rolled edges), wrap your thread twice around the tension dial or guide (Fig. 5.50).

- If, after loosening the tension to 0, you find you need a looser tension (e.g., for heavier pearl cotton or yarn), remove decorative thread from the tension altogether. You may need to place a strip of tape over the slot so the thread does not find its way into the tension. Also check that the decorative thread is not hanging up on a thread guide or around a spool pin (Fig. 5.51).

- If both looper threads hang off the edge of the fabric, widen the stitch.

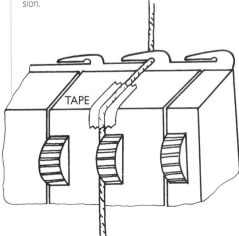

Fig. 5.51: *When using heavier decorative thread on the upper looper, you may need to place a strip of tape over the slot so decorative thread does not find its way into the tension.*

TAPE

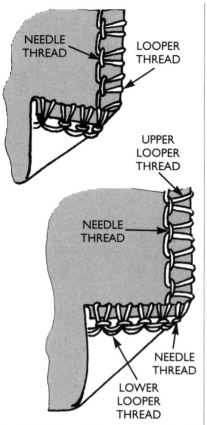

Fig. 5.52: *Stitch a rolled edge on the edge of the fabric so thread wraps the edge.*

NEEDLE THREAD

LOOPER THREAD

UPPER LOOPER THREAD

NEEDLE THREAD

NEEDLE THREAD

LOWER LOOPER THREAD

"Satin Serging" a Narrow Rolled Edge

This edge, commonly found on napkin and scarf edges, is one of the most common serger stitches, but it can take on many decorative looks depending on what thread you use on the upper looper.

Serger Readiness Checklist

Stitch: narrow rolled edge

Foot: narrow rolled edge

Stitch length: short

Stitch width: narrow

Thread: all-purpose serger thread in needle and lower looper; Woolly Nylon in upper looper

Tension: loosen needle slightly from normal; make upper looper very tight; make lower looper moderately tight

Accessories: some models use a rolled hem plate, others move the wide stitch finger out of the way

1. Set your serger for a rolled edge. Some sergers have a built-in rolled hem feature, which you adjust with a lever or dial. Others require changing the foot and/or needle plate. Some sergers have the capability of using two threads for a rolled hem; to adjust it, see your Operating Manual.

2. Stitch a rolled edge on a single or double fabric layer using a tone-on-tone thread so thread wraps the edge (Fig. 5.52).

SCRUNCHING SCHOOL

Scrunching? What's that, you ask? Just one of the easiest ways to create texture there is. Look how designer Sandra Benfield scrunched the foundation fabric under her couched "Fastube Texture" in the Designer Showcase in the color pages.

1. To make an 18" (46cm) square, cut a lightweight all-cotton 21" (53.5cm) square (cotton holds the wrinkle better than synthetic, man-made fibers, or blends).

2. Wet it thoroughly; then scrunch, wrinkle, and ball-up the square, putting a rubber band around it to hold in the wrinkles.

3. Dry the piece naturally or put it in a dryer with a dry towel to speed up the drying process.

4. When the scrunched piece is dry, mount it on an 18" (46cm) square of foundation fabric; muslin, cotton flannel, or fusible knit interfacing work well. Do this by opening the scrunched piece, pull it into the corners and let the wrinkles fall where they may (Fig. 5.53). If you have mounted this onto muslin or flannel, straight stitch around the edges to keep it in place. If you have mounted scrunching to the fusible interfacing, fuse the wrinkles

down. Now you have a textured base as a foundation for couching or bobbin work (see "Couching the Carefree Way" and "Bobbin Work That's Almost Play" earlier in this chapter).

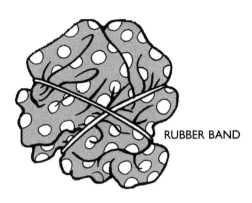

Fig. 5.53: *Open scrunched piece, pull it into the corners and let the wrinkles fall where they may.*

RUBBER BAND

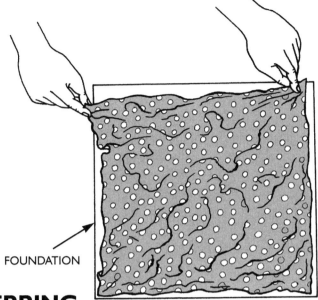

FOUNDATION

TRANSFERRING DESIGNS WITH EASE

You'll need to do two kinds of transferring designs in this book. First, to create the many shirts we've shown, you'll need to make patterns of the shirt's collar, pocket, yoke, and cuff so that you can cut and shape the textured fabrics that will be added to the shirt. This is described in "Creating Garment-Part Patterns." When you want to transfer specific designs used in the textures (such as the Petroglyph Pets in Chapter One), you can use an iron-on transfer pen, a special stitching method, or tracing paper. The photocopy machine is another easy alternative.

Creating Garment-Part Patterns

When adding texture to a particular garment, you'll often find the easiest way to do this is to photocopy the part of the garment to which you will be applying your textures. Then add seam allowances where necessary—voilà, a pattern. If you don't have access to a copy machine, lay the garment down, place a piece of pattern tracing material such as Do-Sew on top of the garment, and trace over the seamlines using a wash-away fabric marker. Add seam allowances, cut out your pattern, then check the fit on the original and make adjustments as needed.

The Heat-Transfer Pen Method

1. Start the flow of ink following the manufacturer's instructions. (We used Sulky Iron-On Transfer Pen with good results.)

2. Draw or trace the design onto a smooth piece of tracing or typing paper.

WATER-SOLUBLE STABILIZER

Fig. 5.54: *Trace your design directly onto water-soluble stabilizer using a dark permanent fine-point Sharpie marker or Pigma pen. Pin stabilizer to the surface of the fabric and follow the lines by stitching through the stabilizer.*

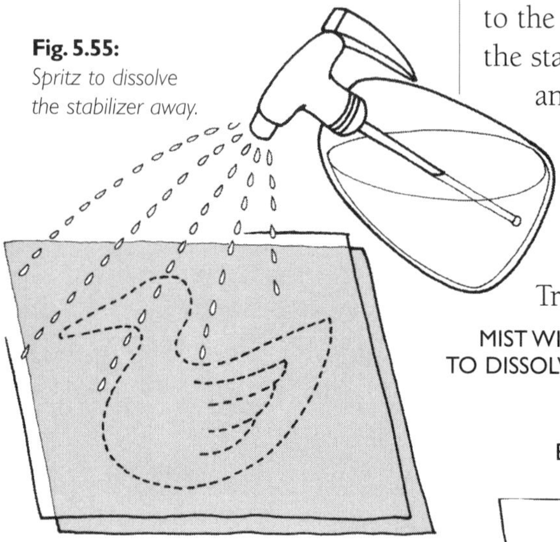

Fig. 5.55:
Spritz to dissolve the stabilizer away.

MIST WITH WATER
TO DISSOLVE STABILIZER

3. Place transfer, ink side down, against the fabric.

4. Hold the transfer in place and press over it with a hot iron, pressing down firmly. Move the iron slightly to avoid an impression under the steam holes.

5. After about 30 seconds and without shifting the transfer pattern, lift a corner to see if the design has transferred to the fabric. If not, reapply the iron.

6. Transfer can be used several more times.

The Stitch-Over Transfer-Design Method

The stitched-over method saves a step because you trace the design directly onto water-soluble stabilizer using a light permanent fine-point Sharpie marker or Pigma pen. Then, simply pin the stabilizer to the surface of the fabric and follow the lines by stitching through the stabilizer (Fig. 5.54). Because we are using dark base fabrics, and the lines are done with permanent ink, the stitches cover the lines and won't show. Wet or spritz the stabilizer away and your embroidery is complete (Fig. 5.55).

The Trace-Over Transfer-Design Method

Trace the design on tracing paper. Lay a piece of dressmaker's carbon over the fabric, carbon side down. Place the traced design over dressmaker's carbon, then draw over the lines using an empty ballpoint pen (Fig. 5.56). Now you are ready to start your texturing technique.

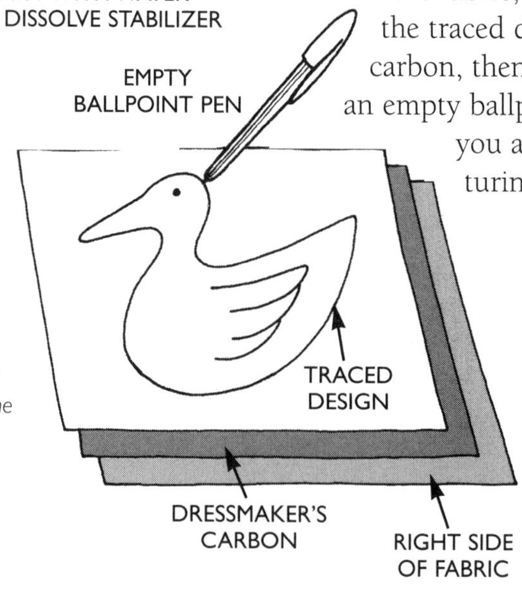

EMPTY
BALLPOINT PEN

TRACED
DESIGN

Fig. 5.56: *Place the traced design over dressmaker's carbon; then draw over the lines using an empty ballpoint pen.*

DRESSMAKER'S
CARBON

RIGHT SIDE
OF FABRIC

TUCKS MADE SIMPLE BY SERGING

Try serging tucks for an interesting textural look used on everything from heirloom sewing to outerwear.

Serger Readiness Checklist

	WIDE TUCKS	*NARROW TUCKS*
• *Stitch:*	balanced three-thread overlock	narrow rolled edge

Wide Tucks (con't)	Narrow Tucks (con't)
• *Foot*: standard	rolled hem
• *Stitch length*: short	same
• *Stitch width*: wide	narrow
• *Needle*: appropriate for fabric and thread	same
• *Thread*: all-purpose sewing thread in needle; #8 pearl cotton, Decor, or Candlelight in upper and lower loopers; or all-purpose serging thread in lower looper	all-purpose serging thread in needle and lower looper; Woolly Nylon in upper looper
• *Miscellaneous*: mid-weight woven fabric	lightweight woven fabric

1. Iron a crease to mark the first tuck. Place the fold of the tuck under the foot between the needle and knives so the stitches form on the fold.

2. Press tucks in one direction so the decorative thread is on top of the fabric (Fig. 5.57). If you have used decorative thread in both loopers, you can press tucks in either direction or alternate directions and stitch them down to make a wave (Fig. 5.58).

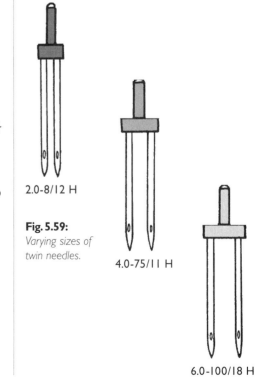

Fig. 5.57: *For regular tucks, use decorative thread in only one of the loopers. Then press the tucks so that the decorative thread shows.*

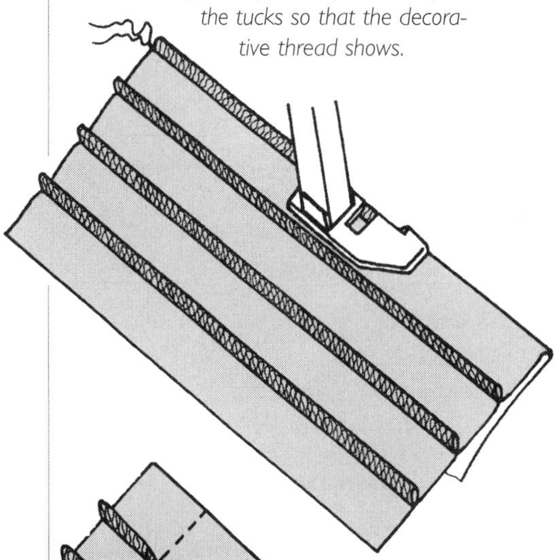

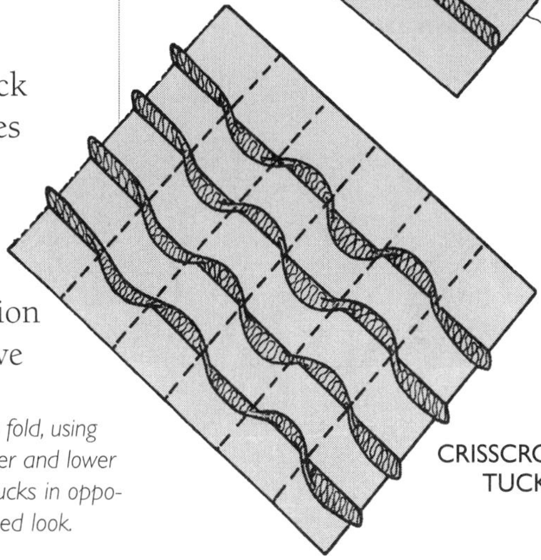

Fig. 5.58: *Serge tucks over a fold, using decorative thread in the upper and lower looper. Press and stitch the tucks in opposite directions for a crisscrossed look.*

CRISSCROSSED TUCKS

TWIN-NEEDLE TEXTURIZING

An effective way to create texture and dimension is with your twin, or double, needle. Made with one shank and two needles fixed to a crossbar, twin needles are sized by two numbers and a letter (Fig. 5.59). For example, a 2.0 80/12 H means the needles are two millimeters apart, are a size 80/12, and have a universal point; a 4.0 90/14 HS means the needles are 4 millimeters apart, are a size 90/14 and have a stretch point. Use narrow needles for pin tucks, wider needles to create a soft ridge, channel, or cable for echo-quilting.

Use twin needles in a machine with a top or front-loading bobbin so the needles sit in the machine properly. While sewing, the bobbin thread zigzags between the top two threads and gently pulls them together, creating a tuck. For a crisper ridge, tighten the upper tension; you can even cord the tuck if your machine has the capabilities (ask your local dealer or see your Operating Manual).

2.0-8/12 H

Fig. 5.59:
Varying sizes of twin needles.

4.0-75/11 H

6.0-100/18 H

Most-Excellent Echo-Quilting

When Jan made a sashiko jacket featuring a special chimpanzee and other animals, she needed a way to tie all the motifs together. She echo-quilted around the shapes using wide twin needles to create an overall texture and a stunning jacket.

Machine Readiness Checklist

Stitch: straight

Foot: embroidery/appliqué

Stitch length: 3-3.5 (8-9 stitches per inch)

Stitch width: 0

Needle: 4.0 90/14 stretch twin

Needle position: center

Thread: white, ivory, or ecru cordonnet or topstitching thread

Tension: loosen top; bobbin, normal

Miscellaneous: pre-shrunk lightweight denim or polished cotton ironed to cotton flannel for foundation

1. Prepare the fabric and foundation as described in "Sashiko Secrets" earlier in this chapter.

2. After testing, begin sewing at an edge and guide a presser foot width away from the appliqué, design, or shape. Try to follow in a smooth, undulating fashion, rather than turning sharp corners.

3. If you need to pivot, stop sewing with the needle in the fabric, but while it's on its way up out of the fabric. In certain instances you can pivot as if pivoting around a single needle without stitch distortion. In other cases, let the needle come just out of the fabric, then pivot. The pivoting needle will form a square and thread from one of the needles will cut diagonally across the square (Fig. 5.60).

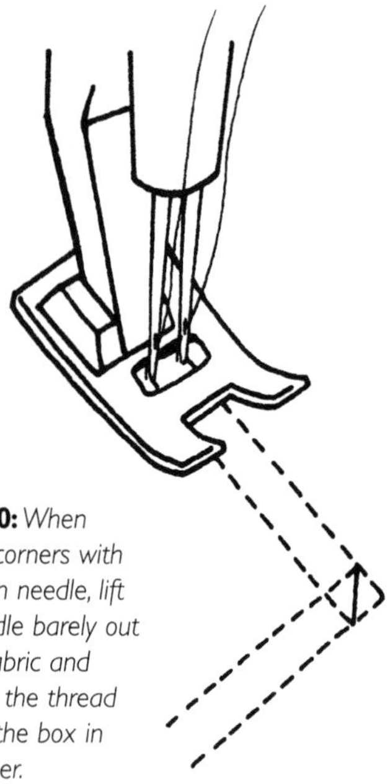

Pintucked Perfection

In the Designer Showcase (see color pages), see how designer Joyce Drexler used her twin needles to make beautiful pintucks in "Go with the Flow."

Machine Readiness Checklist

- *Stitch:* straight
- *Foot:* three- or five-groove pintuck
- *Stitch length:* 2-3 (9-13 stitches per inch)

Fig. 5.60: *When turning corners with your twin needle, lift the needle barely out of the fabric and pivot, so the thread crosses the box in the corner.*

- *Stitch width:* 0
- *Needle:* 2.5 80/12
- *Thread:* all-purpose or cotton sewing thread
- *Tension:* tighten top for desired effect; bobbin, normal
- *Miscellaneous:* disappearing marker and ruler; size five pearl cotton (optional)
- *Fabric suggestions:* lightweight woven cotton such as organdy or cotton shirting

1. If your machine has a hole in the needle plate or a corded pintuck accessory that will accommodate cord, thread the hole or guide with pearl cotton as directed in your Operating Manual.

2. On a scrap, draw a line on the lengthwise grain to mark pin-tuck placement using the disappearing marker and ruler. Sew a test tuck, adjusting the upper tension for the desired effect—for a crisper tuck, tighten the upper tension. If you want to sew a second tuck parallel to the first, turn the fabric around and guide the previous tuck under one of the grooves in the foot (Fig. 5.61).

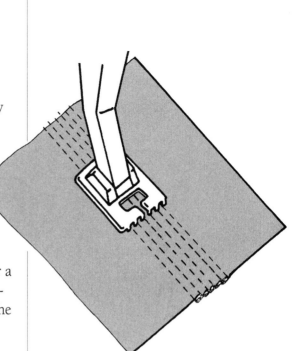

Fig. 5.6 I: *When sewing parallel tucks, use the pintuck foot so grooves of the foot track over the previously-stitched tucks.*

Our "Texturing A to Z" list is by no means all-inclusive. Creative sew-ers and sergers constantly are inventing new texturing techniques or reinventing the old to fit today's new threads, cords, presser feet, fabrics, sewing machines, and sergers. It's an ongoing process, and one of the reasons we love our jobs!

We hope our ideas and those of the contributing designers have been inspirational and have motivated you to get started on your own terrific textures. Whether you worked through the book in order or jumped around, we trust you have enjoyed your textural "tour." What we have discovered, and hope you have too, is that no matter what you try, you can't make a mistake. If you don't like how something turned out on one side of the project, repeat your mistake on the other side, and the world will think you wanted it that way. We hope you'll look for more short subject topics in the *Sew & Serge* book series. Until next time, happy texturing.

—J.D. and J.S.

Designer Showcase Key

Here is a key to the fun and fascinating textures found in the Designer Showcase (see the color pages). Each photo found in the Designer Showcase is shown here in black-and-white, followed by the name, designer, product information, and skill level of each texture in the photo. The designers themselves describe the technique(s) they used and their sources of inspiration, including any other information that will help you create the same embellishment. (If a designer has created more than one texture, her photo appears only with the first texture mentioned. Author photos are found on the About the Authors pages later in the book.)

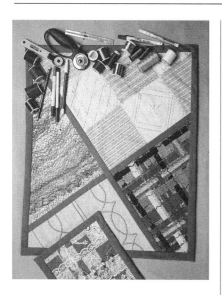

Winging It *(top)*

This was a "make it up as you go" project. A wing needle was appropriate to "winging" the project, so I started there. It needed more dimension, so I changed to a twin needle. Some of the stitches are on top of Ribbon Floss. Basically, I sat in front of my Viking, touched buttons, and winged it.

Product and fabric credits: *Ribbon Floss*

Skill level: *Beginner*

Jill McCloy
*Educational
Consultant
Viking/White
Sewing Machine Co.*

Stripe-Easy-Stitch Wander *(lower right)*

Grosgrain ribbon is woven in a pattern and stitched in place with various built-in stitches. The source of inspiration is looking at cultivated land from an airplane.

Product and fabric credits: *Madeira 40 weight rayon*

Skill level: *Beginner*

Susan Rock
Designer/Instructor

Serged Rolled-Hem Pintuck with Soutache Braid *(bottom)*

For pintuck, fold fabric at tuck line. Press. Set blind hem foot so the guide is just to the right of the needle. Serge the tuck, aligning the fold with the guide on the blind hem foot. Always sew the tuck from the right side of the fabric, so all tucks look the same. This may require you to sew tucks in two dif-

April Dunn
Free-lance Educator

ferent directions (top to bottom and bottom to top) if you want the tucks pressed away from the center.

To make soutache, feed the filler cord in the hole of your presser foot (if your serger has the hole). Serge. The rolled hem will cover the cord as you serge. Attach soutache to fabric with monofilament or matching thread. Thread the novelty chain through the hole of a braiding foot and zigzag the braid in place.

Product and fabric credits: *Signature decorative thread; Signature monofilament; Kauffman fabric; Elna Pro-5DC*

Skill level: *Intermediate*

An Unfinished Piece of Playing *(left)*

Crinkling, dying fabric, and couching techniques are taken from "Texture With Textiles" and "More ... Texture With Textiles."

Product and fabric credits:
Capitol Imports ribbons; Sulky metallic thread: Kreinik braids; Pfaff-Mez thread; Seitec fabric dyes

Skill level: *Intermediate*

Linda McGehee
Author, Publisher, Teacher, Designer

The Wright Stuff *(separate piece at bottom)*

After constructing the fabric using 2" (5cm) squares, I attached a variety of Wright's laces, pearls, motifs, and ribbon roses.

Joellen Reinhardt
Wm. E. Wright Co. Exhibits and Publicity

Product and fabric credits: *Wright's ribbons and trims*

Skill level: *Beginner*

Hangy-Dangy Medallions

(separate circles at upper left)

Cut out a printed shape from your fabric, sandwich it between two layers of plastic stabilizer and place it in a hoop. Use mostly straight stitches around the raw edge of the cut-out at least three times to finish the edges. Then stitch around your cut-out more randomly. Be sure to stitch in the air (through the stabilizer) where there is no fabric, to create more hangy-dangy parts of your design. As you recreate the fabric, get wild with the number and kinds of threads. You can use thread to follow or highlight a certain print pattern in the piece or add color not even in the print. Try making thread tassels that hang off the design, too. Remove stabilizer, press and secure the medallion to your shirt with a straight stitch within the medallion.

April Dunn
Free-lance Educator

Product and fabric credits: *Signature rayon embroidery thread; Speed Cro-Sheen; Elna Diva-9000; Elna Pro-5DC; Hoffman International "Antique Medallions"; Schmetz machine embroidery needle; Lammertz-Metafil needle*

Skill level: *Intermediate*

Primary Pizazz *(top)*

I added a stripe of topstitching-thread stitches from the bobbin, by by-passing the bobbin tension and sewing with the right side of the fabric toward the throat plate. I used lateral zigzag with twin needle.

Product and fabric credits: *YLI Jeans Topstitching Thread (variegated); Sulky embroidery thread (metallic light and dark blue); Totally Stable stabilizer; Esanté Sewing Machine*

Skill level: *Intermediate*

Gretchen Heinlein-Wilson
Baby Lock Educator

Crazy-Eight Fringe
(separate fringe at upper right)

I wanted a fringe-looking trim but not the standard-looking fringe. First I manipulated pinked, bias-cut fabric and cords threaded with silver beads into undulating figure-eight shapes. Then I used an ordinary straight stitch and couched the fringe to adding-machine tape to create a not-too-ordinary looking fringe. The paper tape pulls away for easy application.

Product and fabric credits: *Lily Kountry Kabled Kotton; Western Crafts Metallic Bead Collection*

Skill level: *Beginner*

Grace Johnson
President, Dressing Dynamics

On the Border *(far right)*

These simple border ideas could be used to embellish garments or home decorating projects. They were created by using a combination of decorative stitches common to many machines.

Product and fabric credits: *Coats Metallic and Rayon Specialty Threads*

Skill level: *Beginner*

Lynn Browne
Manager, Educational Programs Coats & Clark

Twix Heaven and Hell *(bottom)*

With ribbon thread on the bobbin, my Elna and I can turn anything into a designer creation.

Product and fabric credits: *Tear-away Metier de Geneve ribbon thread; Madeira metallic thread; Elna sewing machine*

Skill level: *Intermediate*

Angie Jachimowski
Lela's Sewing Machine Centers Manager

Quilted Serger Plaid *(far left)*

Construct the wide braid with a serger. Use novelty thread on the upper looper, thread to coordinate with novelty thread on the lower looper and needle. Set differential feed: $^1/_N$, with tensions for normal balanced three-thread. Stitch over 1-$^1/_4$" Seams Great, then pile the fabrics: top-project fabric, middle-Thermore batting, and bottom-bleached muslin. Pin the serger braid in the desired pattern and stitch in place with a sewing machine. Set serger up for two-thread chain stitching and stitch on either side of the attached braid, using the serger presser foot as a guide.

April Dunn
Free-lance Educator

Product and fabric credits: *Thermore batting; Seams Great; Marcus Brother Cotton; YLI-multicolored "Uncle Sam" Woolly Nylon; red Pearl Crown Rayon; royal blue Designer 6; Elna Pro 5DC; Elna Diva/9000*

Skill level: *Beginner*

Miracles From Memory Craft 8000
(inner upper left)

The fabric and cord were on my sewing table, the red thread already in my machine, so I used all of them. I wanted to show the Miracle Stitcher and design a border using cross stitches with the Cloth Setter. Then I added other decorative stitches.

Product and fabric credits: *Needloft metallic cord by Uniek; New Home Acrylic thread; Vanish Away stabilizer; New Home Memory Craft 8000 and Memory Card #15; Cloth Setter; Miracle Stitcher*

Mary Carollo
New Home Sewing Machine Educator

Skill level: *Intermediate to Advanced*

Decorating the Edges and Between
(inner upper right)

Using satin ribbon and rayon thread, edges of the cotton strips are joined decoratively. Decorative stitches embellish plain fabric strips and the round (use circular attachment) flower.

Product and fabric credits: *Metafil needle #80; Sulky Rayon thread*

Amy Doggett
Education Consultant Viking Sewing Machine Co.

Skill level: *Intermediate to Advanced*

Just Doodling Around *(inner middle right)*

I scrunched fabric, bonded it to Easy Knit fusible interfacing with my Elna Press, then decorated it with $^1/_8$" (3mm) wide ribbon and rayon machine embroidery thread.

Product and fabric credits: *$^1/_8$" (3mm) wide Offray Spool O'Ribbon; Easy Knit fusible interfacing; Coats & Clark rayon thread*

Diana Cedolia
Sew Better Seminars Instructor

Skill level: *Intermediate*

Potpourri *(inner lower right)*

Several fabrics are used as well as many techniques on both sewing machine and serger: flatlocking; sashiko; and pleating. Flatlock joins and enhances colors of the fabrics. Metallic threads glisten and attract the eye.

Product and fabric credits:
YLI Pearl Crown Rayon; Sulky Metallic Thread

Skill level: *Beginner*

Dori Nanry
Baby Lock Educator

Hodge-Podge Excitement *(inner lower left)*

You asked for it! It includes ruched Caress fabric, charted needle, fringe-foot flowers, and decorative stitches. Yes, it's hodge-podge — I do get over-enthusiastic.

Product and fabric credits: *Caress fabric; Sulky rayon and metallic threads*

Skill level: *All*

Marilyn Gatz
Sew Better Seminars Instructor

Hot Stuff Lace *(upper left)*

Hot Stuff! allows the creative sew-er complete freedom. It's the only stabilizer that will allow you to create lace insets, appliqués, or create your own fabric without a hoop. Create a square grid of stitching first; then cover it with circles of free stitching using a darning foot or spring needle without a presser foot.

Product and fabric credits: *Natesh rayon machine embroidery thread; Hot Stuff!*

Skill level: *All*

Deborah Casteel
Aardvark Adventures Owner

PHOTO COURTESY OF GLAMOUR SHOTS

Woven Wonder *(upper middle)*

I saw this done on a designer dress in a local department store and wanted to duplicate it on a jacket sleeve I'll make myself. I intentionally didn't seam the 5" (13cm) strips because I didn't want the bulk or ridge created by the seam to show through. Each strip is folded and pressed the long way, and after weaving, I'll fuse it together using a lightweight interfacing.

Product and fabric credits: *Fray Check*

Skill level: *Beginner*

Cathie Moore
Sew Better Seminars Administrative

PHOTO COURTESY OF GLAMOUR SHOTS

Glamour Vest *(upper right)*

I placed 100% pre-washed cotton flannel behind the sueded rayon fabric and then couched down the chains, which I serged (set serger for rolled hem and make rolled hem chain with Madeira Glamour in the upper looper and matching thread in the needle and lower looper). After cutting out the garment, I constructed it on the sewing machine, using conventional methods.

Product and fabric credits: *Madeira Glamour*

Skill level: *All*

Patsy Shields
*Sew Better
Seminars Instructor
Patsy Shields
Seminars*

Fun With Fiber-Etch *(lower right)*

I purchased flocked appliqués and ironed them on to 100% cotton to produce "cutwork without cutting" using Fiber-Etch fabric removing gel.

Product and fabric credits: *Fiber-Etch fabric remover gel*

Skill level: *Beginner*

Michele Hester
*Silkpaint
Corporation
President*

Wild Bill Rides Again! *(lower left)*

I was inspired by glancing at an old wild west book of my husband's, which showed Buffalo Bill wearing a terrific pair of buckskin gloves. Leather and denim have been partners for so long! Chamois (being washable) is my first choice. Cut the square, then draw a 3" (7.6cm) border on all four sides and stitch in a twin needle border on the drawn line. Cut fringe up to the stitching. Rows of decorative stitching, curving pintucks and random beading with monofilament thread finished off the piece. I love it! It moves, has texture and interest. This technique is perfect for yoke, collar, or cuff treatments.

Nancy Bednar
*Bernina of America
Sewing Specialist*

PHOTO COURTESY OF BRESNAHAN STUDIO

Product and fabric credits: *Chamois (available at auto parts and hardware stores); rayon machine embroidery thread; tear-away stabilizer*

Skill level: *Advanced Beginner to Intermediate*

Hearts and Flowers *(far left and far right)*

Victorian quilts have always inspired me with their use of hand-embroidery. With decorative stitches on the machine, it's a natural for embellishment. I drew "blocks" first, did decorative stitches in each section, and stitched over the lines last. A topstitching needle is essential to accommodate the Renaissance thread.

Product and fabric credits: *Pfaff American Sales Corp.; Sew-Art International Renaissance thread*

Skill level: *Beginner*

Linnette Whicker
Pfaff Educational Consultant

Go With the Flow *(top)*

I wanted to create depth while also allowing for 3-D texture. The twin needle 4.0 size gave me the extension I was after. Batting and stipple quilting between the raised areas gave different relief and brilliance from the Sulky Sliver. The fabric I chose gave the project the flow and color shading I wanted. It reminded me of the look of water in the Gulf when viewing it from an airplane window.

Product and fabric credits: *Sulky Sliver metallic thread #8017 and #8050; fabric by Nancy Crow for John Kaldor; cotton classic by Fairfield Processing*

Skill level: *Beginner*

Joyce Drexler
Sulky of America and Speed Stitch Inc. Co-owner

Fastube Texture *(middle)*

My inspiration came from Linda F. McGehee's book, *More Texture with Textiles*. I used lattice piecing with tubes in spliced areas.

Product and fabric credits: *Sulky metallic thread; Easy Knit interfacing, Fasturn*

Skill level: *Beginner to Intermediate*

Sandra Benfield
Crowning Touch Designer

A Trunk Show *(bottom)*

I was very excited about cut-a-way appliqué after reading Linda Fry Kenzle's *Embellishments*. The inspiration for this piece was the Hoffman fabric. I love the elephants I layered four fabrics — from bottom layer up: elephants, purple satin, gold dotted black tulle, and geometric shapes. From the underside I straight-stitched to outline the elephants. From the top, I cut down to expose the

Jan Nunn
Sew Better Seminars Instructor

elephants. Then I used decorative threads to straight stitch — and in some cases zigzag — around the geometric shapes. I clipped down through one and two layers to expose the purple or tulle. Then I played with a variety of metallic threads from my stash to embellish the geometric shapes and elephants. Once I start, it's hard to stop! So I sat all day — sewing the time away — happy as a jay!

Product and fabric credits: *Hoffman fabric (top and bottom layer); Tinsel, Signature metallic, Madeira Glamour, and YLI Candlelight threads*

Skill level: *All*

Quilted Cowgirl *(upper left)*

Add dimensional texture to an already printed fabric with pintucking and quilting. Then add fringe, buttons, and cord made on the sewing machine or serger to complete the look.

Jackie Dodson
Author
Product and Fabric Credits: *Ultrasuede; Sulky thread*
Skill Level: *Beginner*

Fringin' and Bobbin Along *(upper right)*

Add texture to almost any project by putting the too-big-for-the-needle cord in the bobbin. We call this bobbin work or cabling. Add bits of lace and buttons for more texture. The fringe around the collar is made on a fringe fork; the collar is outlined with serger braid.

Jackie Dodson
Author
Product and fabric credits: *DMC Pearl Cotton; Offray ribbon; Wonder Thread monofilament; Ribbon Floss*
Skill Level: *Beginner to Intermediate*

Guatemalan Cowpoke Vest *(lower right)*

This vest was a lot of fun to make because I used so many different techniques, everything from piping and ribbon tucks to Texas Mink Fringe and Blooming Fabric. I also used variegated embroidery thread and my favorite decorative stitches to embellish the stripes.

Jan Saunders
Author
Product and Fabric Credits: *Short vest pattern (I used Dos de Tejas #6022 "Fringe Benefits"); Sliver or flat Tinsel Stream Lamé; Offray ribbon; Perfect Pleater pleater board*
Skill Level: *Intermediate*

Classy Cowboy Vest *(lower middle)*

When I found this fabric, I had to buy it — I loved it. When Viking called to ask if I'd make a vest for their trunk show, everything came together: my fabric, my boxes of pseudo-leathers, and some designs I'd been doodling. Appliqués are attached with blanket stitches; the lining of the vest is covered with Pictogram and Omnigram designs to mimic the appliqués. I liked it so much I made another vest for myself. The original vest was featured in Vogue Patterns magazine (May/June 1994) and offered as a Viking/Vogue pattern.

Jackie Dodson
Author

Product and fabric credits: *Sulky rayon machine embroidery thread; HTC Armo Weft fusible interfacing and Trans-Web fusible web; Viking sewing machine #1 with Pictogram and Omnigram cassettes*

Skill level: *Intermediate*

Mola in Reverse (lower left)

I was inspired by a mola I picked up in Puerto Rico. I had always wanted to try reverse appliqué and then I came up with a surface-detail variation that is much faster. The simple tapered satin stitches mimic the look of the reverse appliqué mola shapes. The vest is reversible, with decorative stitching inside, too. I used piping around the collar, armholes, and inside. This vest, along with Jackie's Classy Cowboy, was selected as one of the "Very Viking Vests in Vogue" featured in Vogue Patterns magazine (May/June 1994) and offered as a Viking/Vogue pattern.

Jan Saunders
Author

Product and fabric credits: *Coats and Clark quilting thread*

Skill level: *Beginner*

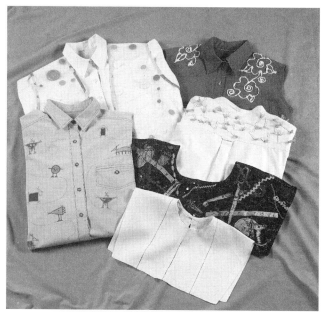

Linen Collar (bottom right)

The linen in this collar started out as four pieces. I fagotted the pieces together, pressed the seams open, and secured the seams with a tone-on-tone decorative stitch. I then staystitched around the neckline to secure the fagotting stitches so they wouldn't unravel when I cut out the neckline. To finish the collar, I mitered the corners and hemmed it. Then I hem-stitched about an inch (2.5cm) from the hem edge using a wing needle; an elongated elastic straight stitch; and darning thread, top and bobbin. I finished the neckline with bias tape and a snap.

Jan Saunders
Author

Product and fabric credits: *Coats & Clark embroidery thread*

Skill level: *Intermediate*

Sources of Supplies

Please ask your sewing-machine or fabric dealer to order any product she or he doesn't stock. If you do not have access to a complete store, try mail order. As a courtesy, please include a self-addressed stamped envelope when inquiring. While we have tried to be accurate and complete, addresses change, businesses move or die, and we make regrettable omissions by mistake. Please send updates to us in care of Open Chain Publishing, P.O. Box 2364-P, Menlo Park, CA 94026.

Aardvark Adventures
P.O. Box 2449
Livermore, CA 94551
Stabilizers, shisha mirrors, three-fold needlework, cards, and a few other supplies. Call or write for more information. (800) 388-2687.

Air-Lite Synthetics Mfg., Inc.
342 Irwin Street
Pontiac, MI 48341-2982
Simplicity quilt batting, Fiberfil, pillow forms, urethane foam rolls, quilt batting on rolls, Comfort Fil 7 (Polargard) continuous filament batting, poly-insulate quilt batting.

Aleene's
Division of Artis, Inc.
Buellton, CA 93427
Glues, Stop Fraying, Tack-It.

ARTFABR!K
664 W. Main Street
Cary, IL 60013
Hand-dyed fabric and thread. Send an SASE to receive fabric and thread prices. Thread card $7.00. (708) 639-5966 or (708) 931-7684.

Bernina of America, Inc.
3500 Thayer Court
Aurora, IL 60504-6182
Bernina and Bernette sewing machines and sergers, plus accessories.

Brother International Corp.
200 Cottontail Lane
Somerset, NJ 08875
Sewing machines and Homelock sergers.

Clotilde, Inc.
2 Sew Smart Way
Stevens Point, WI 54481-80301
Perfect Pleater pleater board, sewing notions catalog.

CM Offray & Son, Inc.
P.O. Box 601
Chester, NJ 07930
Quality ribbons.

Coats & Clark
30 Patewood Drive, Suite 351
Greenville, SC 29615
Coats Dual Duty Plus for Overlock, Transparent Nylon Monofilament, Metallic, and Rayon thread.

Concord House
1359 Broadway
New York, NY 10018
Multi-purpose fabrics for apparel, bridal, quilting, home decorating, and crafts.

Crowning Touch Inc.
2410 Glory C Road
Medford, OR 97501
Fasturn and Fastube Sewing Foot.

DMC
107 Trumbull Street
Elizabeth, NJ 07206
Embroidery threads and pearl cotton.

Dritz Corp.
P.O. Box 5028
Spartanburg, SC 29304
Stitch Witchery, Hem-N-Trim, Disappearing Ink Marking Pen, Fray Check, and Sewing/Craft Glue Stick.

Elna, Inc.
7642 Washington Avenue South
Eden Prairie, MN 55344
Elna and Elnita sewing machines, Elnalock sergers, Elnapress, Amazing Trace Embroiderer, notions, accessories, and Ribbon Thread.

Fabric Traditions
1350 Broadway
New York, NY 10018
Multi-purpose fabrics for apparel, quilting, home decorating, and crafts.

Fabulous Fur
Donna Salyers
700 Madison Avenue
Covington, KY 41011
Man-made furs and leather, sewing how-to books, videos, related patterns, and notions. Free catalog.

Fairfield Processing Corp.
88 Rose Hill Avenue
P.O. Drawer 1157
Danbury, CT 06810
Products include four types of fiberfill (Poly-Fil, Poly-Fil Supreme, Crafter's Choice, and EZ Stuff), four bonded and two needlepunch battings in a variety of sizes. Call (800) 243-0989 for nearest retail store in your area.

Fiskars Manufacturing Corp.
7811 W. Stewart Avenue
Wausau, WI 54401
Rotary cutter with straight, pinking, and wave blades, cutting mats, shears, scissors, and rulers.

G Street Fabric
12240 Wilkins Avenue
Rockville, MD 20852
Mail order fabrics, free swatch service.
(800) 333-9191.

Gingher, Inc.
P.O. Box 8865
Greensboro, NC 27419
Top quality scissors, shears,
and thread snips.

Global Village Imports
1101 SW Washington, Suite 140
Portland, OR 97205-2313
Handwoven 100% cotton fabrics
and trim from Guatemala.

Gutermann of America, Inc.
8227 Arrowridge Boulevard
Charlotte, NC 28273
Hand and machine sewing threads;
cone threads for sergers; and heavy
duty topstitching, metallic, silk, upholstery,
and cotton quilting threads.

Handler Textile Corp.
24 Empire Boulevard
Moonachie, NJ 07074
Armo Weft, Touch 'O Gold, Rinsaway,
Easy Stitch, Trans-Web Tape,
Fuse-A-Craft, and HTC Fusible Fleece.

Hoffman California Fabrics
25792 Obrero Drive
Mission Viejo, CA 92691
Fashion, quilting, and decorator fabrics.

Hollywood Trims Inc.
42005 Cook Street
Palm Desert, CA 92260
Decorator trims and tassels.

Jehlor Fantasy Fabrics
730 Andover Park West
Seattle, WA 98188
Lamé, trims, beads, and sequins.
Catalog $5 (refundable with order
of $50 or more). (206) 575-8520.

JHB International Inc.
1955 South Quince Street
Denver, CO 80231
Fashion, bridal, pearl, holiday, children's,
and men's blazer buttons; jewelry findings;
eyes; charms; thimbles; sweetheart labels.

Jones Tones
68743 Perez Road
Cathedral City, CA 92234
Fabric paints and glues that stretch with
the fabrics to which they are applied.

Juki America, Inc.
3555 Lomita Boulevard., Suite HI
Torrance, CA 90505
Jukilock sergers.

June Tailor, Inc.
P.O. Box 208
Richfield, WI 53076
Rotary cutters, boards, mats, appliqué
mats, and pressing and ironing equipment.
(800) 844-5400.

Kittrich
4500 District Boulevard
Los Angeles, CA 90058
Iron-on Clear Cover, self-adhesive vinyl,
and fabric decorative coverings.

S.H. Kunin Felt Co. Inc./Foss
   Marketing
380 LaFayette Road
Hampton, NH 03842-5000
Classic Rainbow Felt, Prestige Felt and
Holiday Felt; Rainbow Plush Craft Fur;
display fabric; Presto felt squares (just
cut, peel, and stick); Presto letters and
numbers.

Madeira Marketing LTD
600 East 9th Street
Michigan City, IN 46360
Decorative machine and serger threads.
(219) 873-1000.

Mill Creek Fabrics
295 Fifth Avenue
New York, NY 10016
Multi-purpose fabrics for apparel,
home decorating, and crafts.

Mundial Inc.
50 Kerry Place
Norwood, MA 02062
Appliqué scissors, embroidery scissors,
and clippers.

Nancy's Notions
333 Beichl Avenue
Beaver Dam, WI 53916-0683
Specialty presser feet, adhesives,
elastics, and sewing catalog.

National Thread & Supply Corp.
695 Red Oak Road, Dept. A-202
Stockbridge, GA 30281
Threads, pressing equipment, notions.
(800) 331-7600, ext. A-202.

New Home Sewing Machine
100 Hollister Road
Teterboro, NJ 07608
Sewing machines, Mylock sergers,
specialty presser feet and accessories.
(201) 440-8080.

Newark Dressmaker Supply
P.O. Box 20730
Lehigh Valley, PA 18002-0730
Mail order for sewing supplies.
Free catalog. (215) 837-7500.

Pellon Division
Freudenberg Nonwovens
1040 Avenue of the Americas
New York, NY 10018
Wonder Under, Heavy-Duty Wonder
Under, Sof-Shape, Easy-Knit,
Stitch-n-Tear, Pellon Fusible Fleece.

Pfaff Sewing Machine Co.
610 Winters Avenue
Paramus, NJ 07653
Pfaff sewing machines and Hobbylock
sergers, PC Designer Software.

Quality Braid Corp./Sequins
International Inc.
60-01 31st Avenue
Woodside, NY 11377
Braids, sequins, cross-locked beads, fringe.
Call for store closest to you carrying these
products. (718) 204-0002.

Quilters' Resource Inc.
P.O. Box 14885
Chicago, IL 60614
Silk ribbons, French ribbons, trim, antique
buttons and embellishments, 100% silk
thread, patterns, books, unusual notions.

Rhode Island Textile Co.
P.O. Box 999
Pawtucket, RI 02861
Ribbon Floss.

Riccar America
c/o Tacony
1760 Gilsinn Lane
Fenton, MO 63026
Riccar sewing machines and sergers.

Rosebar Textile Co., Inc.
93 Entin Road
Clifton, NJ 07014
Elegant fabrics, including satin.

Sew Art International
P.O. Box 550
Bountiful, UT 84010
Unusual threads for machine embroidery, the Fringe Fork. (800) 231-2787.

Sewing Emporium
1079 Third Avenue
Chula Vista, CA 91910
Notions, presser feet, accessories. Catalog $4.95 (refundable with first order). (619) 420-3490.

Signature
P.O. Box 507
Mount Holly, NC 28120
All-purpose and specialty threads.

Silkpaint Corporation
18220 Waldron Drive
P.O. Box 18
Waldron, MO 64092-0018
Fiber-Etch fabric remover and complete supplies for painting on silk. Telephone (816) 891-7774.

Singer Sewing Co.
135 Raritan Center Parkway
Edison, NJ 08837-3642
Singer sewing machines, Ultralock sergers, Magic Steam Press.

Springs Industries
123 N. White Street
P.O. Box 70
Fort Mills, SC 29715
Crafts, home-dec, and quilted fabrics.

Springs Industries
104 W. 40th Street
New York, NY 10018
Ultrasuede and related fabrics.

Sterns Technical Textiles Co.
100 Williams Street
Cincinnati, OH 45215
Mountain Mist products.

Streamline Industries Inc.
845 Stewart Avenue
Garden City, NY 11530
Buttons, buckles, ribbons, ribbon bows, crests, and appliqués.

Sulky of America
3113D Broadpoint Drive
Harbor Heights, FL 33983
Sulky rayon and metallic thread, Solvy (water-soluble stabilizer), Totally Stable, Heat Away Stabilizer, and Iron-On Transfer Pen.

Sullivan's USA Inc.
224 Williams Street
Bensenville, IL 60106
Sullivan's notions, adhesives, Fix Velour Hook and Loop Tape, zippers, Fray Stoppa.

Swiss-Metrosene Inc.
1107 Martin Drive
Roseville, CA 97661
General purpose threads, cotton machine embroidery threads, and cordonnet.

Tacony Corp.
1760 Gilsinn Lane
Fenton, MO 63026
Baby Lock Sergers (Éclipse) and sewing machines (Esanté); Simplicity sewing machines and sergers; Pattern-Life to reinforce and stabilize paper patterns; notions and accessories.

Tandy Leather Co.
P.O. Box 791
Fort Worth, TX 76101
Leather, suede, beads, laces, and patterns. Catalog $1.00.

Taylor Bedding
P.O. Box 979
Taylor, TX 76570-0979
Batting and pillow forms.

Therm O Web
770 Glenn Avenue
Wheeling, IL 60090
HeatnBond Original and HeatnBond Lite fusibles.

Tinsel Threads, Inc.
Horn of America
P.O. Box 608
Sutton, WV 26601
Machine embroidery rayon and metallic threads.

Treadleart
25834 Narbonne Avenue
Lomita, CA 90717
Sewing and machine embroidery threads, presser feet. Catalog $3 (refundable with $20 order). (310) 534-5122.

V.I.P. Fabrics
1412 Broadway
New York, NY 10018
Multi-purpose fabrics for apparel, quilting, home decorating, and crafts.

VWS
11760 Berea Road
Cleveland, OH 44111
Viking and White sewing machines, Viking Huskylock sergers, White Superlock sergers, specialty presser feet, and accessories.

Web of Thread
3240 Lone Oak Road
Suite 124
Paaducah, Ky 42003
Specialty threads, yarn, ribbon, and cords for the needleartist. Color cards. Catalog (800) 955-8185.

Wm. E. Wright Ltd.
85 South Street
West Warren, MA 01092
Laces, trims, woven ribbons, wire-edge ribbons, embroidered and sequin appliqués, collars, tapes and braids, Bondex, Boye Needles.

Y.L.I.
482 N. Freedom Boulevard
Provo, UT 84601
Designer 6 decorative rayon thread, Woolly Plus heavyweight Woolly Nylon thread, monofilament nylon thread, and Perfect Sew universal needle threader and needle inserter.

About the Authors

Jackie Dodson

Prolific author Jackie Dodson lives in a La Grange Park, Illinois, home stuffed with fabric, yarn, beads, books, sewing machines, sergers — and a patient husband. She earned a Bachelor of Arts degree from Carthage College and attended the University of Iowa and Wisconsin State Teachers' College. Previously employed as a high school teacher, Jackie is now a full-time writer and designer. She is the author or co-author of eleven books in the *Know Your Sewing Machine* series, co-author of *Gifts Galore,* author of *Twenty Easy Machine-Made Rugs, How to Make Soft Jewelry, Quick Quilted Home Decor with your Sewing Machine, Quick Quilted Home Decor with your Bernina Sewing Machine,* and co-author, with Jan Saunders, of *Sew & Serge Pillows! Pillows! Pillows!*

She is a member of the following associations: Hinsdale Embroiderers' Guild; DuPage Textile Arts Guild; American Sewing Guild; Council of American Embroiderers; and Textile, Clothing, and Related Arts Forum. She has appeared on the popular *Sewing with Nancy* and *The Art of Sewing* television programs and has written numerous magazine and newsletter articles, including regular columns for The American Sewing Guild in Chicago, *The Needlework Times,* and *The Creative Machine Newsletter.* Viking/Vogue recently featured her embellished vest in *Vogue Patterns* magazine and made a pattern available.

Jackie has also conducted lectures and seminars for guilds, sewing machine dealers, fabric stores, and national sewing and craft organizations.

In her spare time Jackie enjoys sewing for fun, and spending time with her family at their vacation home in northern Wisconsin.

After her guest semester at the New York Fashion Institute of Technology in New York City, Jan Saunders graduated with a B.A. in home economics, secondary education, and business from Adrian College, Adrian, Michigan. Saunders has spent the last 22 years sharing her flair for fashion and love for sewing with home sew-ers nationwide.

Formerly the education director of a major sewing machine company and of the largest fabric chain in the United States, this Swiss-trained specialist has handled company public relations, developed marketing plans and educational materials, written teaching curriculum and company newsletters, and conducted sales training and sewing seminars nationwide. As the former National Program Director for the Sew Better Seminars program, Jan managed a national team of sewing and serging specialists who taught fashion sewing, serging, wearable art, and home decorating seminars to consumers across the country.

In 1980, her first book, *Speed Sewing* became a Book-of-the-Month selection. Since then she has written the best-selling *Sew, Serge, Press* (Chilton, 1989), and the *Teach Yourself to Sew Better* four-book series (Chilton, 1990–1993). In her most recent book, *Jan Saunders' Wardrobe Quick-Fixes* (Chilton, 1995), she shares industry secrets and offers readers quick practical suggestions on how to embellish, repair, and care for their clothing. Jan has also co-authored *Sew & Serge Pillows, Pillows, Pillows!* with Jackie Dodson, due out this year. Also look for Jan's regular contributions to *Serger Update, Sewing Update, The Creative Machine Newsletter, Sew News,* and *Threads.*

In her spare time, Jan enjoys sewing for pleasure, sailing, cross-country and downhill skiing, classical music, and spending time with her husband Ted, and son Todd.

Jan Saunders

Index